TABLE OF CONTENTS

FOREWORD

Five years ago, I decided that, to best serve the readers of the *Ottawa Citizen's* Food section, we needed a column devoted to microwave cooking. After all, well over 60 percent of Canadian homes had microwave ovens and home cooks, I believed, needed to know more about these "new" machines than how to heat coffee or thaw frozen foods.

I had met Pam Collacott a couple of years before, attending one of her famed "Dinner at Eight" classes. I was very impressed with how organized she was and how delicious her food tasted. And, unlike some "serious cooks," Pam didn't seem to have a temperamental bone in her body. Remaining cool under stress – whether that stress is caused by a fallen soufflé or a culinary *prima donna* – is a Pam Collacott trademark. So when I was given the okay to hire a microwave columnist, Pam was my first choice.

Since she joined the *Citizen's* Food section in 1986, Pam has taught me – and all our readers – a lot about how food reacts in microwave ovens. She has done this through her microwave hints which often appear at the end of each "New Wave Cooking" column, through her excellent recipes and through her joyous enthusiasm for all things culinary.

Over the years I have come to rely on those fine qualities as much as I have on her good cooking. I think that constant readers of the Food section will be delighted to have many of their favourites in one easy-to-reach volume. As for those of you who have never discovered Pam before, you have a real treat in store.

Kathleen Walker
Food Writer, *The Ottawa Citizen*

ACKNOWLEDGEMENTS

This book has been "under construction" for some time, so there are many people that I would like to thank for their help.

Read, Amy and Brian Collacott – from the time I started writing the "New Wave Cooking" column, you have been patient recipe-test guinea pigs and my best critics. You always have positive comments and suggestions, even when my experiments are less than edible. I really appreciate your loving support and your terrific senses of humour!

Kathleen Walker – thank you for going to bat for me when the opportunity to write the "New Wave Cooking" column first came up. You have been such a great help and inspiration to me over the years, and I appreciate your support and value your friendship.

Dorothy Searles – Mom, by example, you gave me your enthusiasm and love of cooking. Many of your delicious recipes which I was able to adapt to microwave appear in this book!

Anne Lindsay – thank you for you friendship and generous sharing of knowledge.

Elizabeth Baird – Your knowledge and enthusiasm for food and friends are a joy to behold. I appreciate the challenges you have offered to me, and Read and I both value your friendship.

Thanks to these food writers and teachers whose recipes appear in this book.
Leslie Beal Bloom – *Barbecue – Sizzling Fire Know-How* (The American Cooking Guild)
Margaret Fraser – *The Canadian Living Microwave Cookbook* (Random House)
Norene Gilletz – *The Microwave Bible* (Warner Books)
Doris Grant – microwave cooking teacher, Ottawa Board of Education
Margie Kreschollek – *The Guaranteed Goof-Proof Microwave Cookbook* (Bantam Books)
Anne Lindsay – *The Lighthearted Cookbook* (Key Porter Books)
Barb Holland and Roxanne McQuilkin – *Microwave Cooking With Style* (McGraw-Hill Ryerson)
Glenda James – *Master Your Microwave* (Mainly Microwave)

Members of the International Association of Culinary Professionals – a network of "food friends" around the world, always there with help, inspiration and friendship.

To Gail, Wendy and Debbie at Creative Bound Inc. Working with you on this project has been a pleasure. Thanks for your help.

To Betty Shields, Connie McCalla and other Betty's Kitchen staff who always have answers to my microwave questions.

To my friends, especially Mary Louise Purdy, my treasured assistant at the Trillium Cooking School, and Wendy Sinclair who suggested indexing the Helpful Hints, and relatives (especially my sisters Cathy, Debbie, Karen and Mary Pat, and my mother-in-law, Enid – dauntless booksellers all!) who shared their recipes and microwave "adventures" with me, and who responded with such enthusiasm to the idea of this book.

Special thanks to the "New Wave Cooking" readers who took the time to write to me with problems and suggestions over the past five years. Please continue to stay in touch! Now you can throw out all those crumpled old newspaper columns and cook from this book!

If your favourite "New Wave Cooking" recipe is not in this book, let me know – I'll be sure to include it in Volume 2!

Pam Collacott

Getting Acquainted with Your Microwave

All microwaves are not created equal, so it is very important that you become familiar with your own oven. Each manufacturer has his own brand of microwave terminology. Once you understand how your oven works, microwave cooking will be much easier for you.

Use the manufacturer's manual/cookbook to answer the following questions:

Δ What is the wattage of your oven?
Δ How many power levels does it have?
Δ Does it have a built-in turntable?
Δ What are its other special features?

Wattage
Cooking times vary with the wattage of the oven. Lower wattage means longer cooking times. 600 to 700 watts is average. If the wattage of your oven is lower than 600, you will probably have to increase the cooking times given in this book. All recipes in this book were tested in a 700 watt oven with a built-in turntable.

Power Levels
Most microwave ovens have variable power levels ranging from High (Full, 100%) to Medium (usually 50%) to Warm (10%). Defrost, which is found on most ovens, is usually 35% power. Using the correct power level to cook food will mean the difference between success and failure in many cases.

Safety Considerations
Never run your microwave empty. If there is a chance that it might be turned on accidentally, leave a glass dish or cup of water in the oven at all times. Teach your children to operate the microwave correctly and safely. It is a safer appliance for them to use than a regular oven or stovetop. Be sure to show them (preferably by marking the dish) which dishes are safe for use in a microwave oven.

When cooking time is long, the heat from the food may transfer to the container, so use oven mitts to handle containers coming out of the microwave.

Steam builds up during cooking in containers which are tightly covered with plastic wrap. Be cautious when removing the plastic, and move away from the escaping steam. Keep the door of the microwave clean and free from food build-up. Never attempt to operate the oven if the door latch is damaged.

Turntable
If your oven does not have a built-in turntable, you may need to rotate food partway through cooking time. This is not always mentioned in a recipe, so get into the habit of

checking partway through cooking time to determine if food needs to be stirred or dishes rotated. Each oven is different, so you must learn what works best as you get to know your oven.

DETERMINING LENGTH OF COOKING TIME

Use the cooking charts in your microwave oven manual/cookbook to determine correct cooking time. The first time that you cook a food, use less time than is recommended, and check for doneness. You can always add a few more seconds, but you cannot always salvage overcooked food.

The larger the quantity of food cooked, the longer the cooking time.

Foods which are very thick or dense will take longer to cook than less dense foods. (for example, meat)

Foods high in sugar or fat cook more quickly than foods with less of these ingredients, as microwaves are attracted to sugar and fat.

STANDING TIME

10% of microwave cooking takes place after the food comes out of the oven, so most recipes include recommended standing time to finish cooking. You should therefore not be alarmed when food looks underdone at the end of cooking time. Check for doneness AFTER recommended standing time, and add more cooking time if needed.

FOR EVEN COOKING RESULTS

Food pieces (meat, vegetables, fish, etc.) should be the same size and shape.

Arrange food pieces in a circle in the cooking dish, leaving the center of the dish empty whenever possible. Food cooks from the outside toward the center.

Stir foods such as vegetables partway through cooking time to move the less-cooked pieces from the center toward the outside edge of the dish.

If the thickness of food pieces is uneven, arrange the pieces so that the thickest part is facing the outer edge of the dish.

Foods cook more evenly in round containers than in square ones.

MICROWAVE-SAFE COOKWARE INCLUDES:

Δ heat-resistant glassware, including measuring cups, bakeware, mixing bowls and serving dishes. Do the cooking in microwave-safe serving dishes and shorten clean-up time!
Δ microwave-safe plastic cookware. Most pieces that can be used in the microwave will have this information printed somewhere on the dish.
Δ cooking bags designed for microwave and regular oven use. Be sure to leave an air vent

to allow steam to escape. Do not use metal twist ties to secure the bags. If a plastic tie is not provided, use a piece of string to close the bag.

Δ most pottery dishes.

To be sure that your pottery and other cookware is safe, use the following test:

CAN THIS DISH BE USED IN THE MICROWAVE ?

If you are unsure about the safety of a dish, place it in the microwave with a glass measure containing 1 cup (250 mL) of water. Microwave on High for 2 minutes, or until water boils. If the dish is still cool to the touch, it is not absorbing microwaves and can be used safely.

For short cooking times you can use wicker baskets, wooden bowls or paper plates.

Small amounts of aluminum foil can be used to shield parts of food that might overcook. The pieces should be small, and should not touch the walls of the microwave, or arcing will result.

COOKWARE TO AVOID INCLUDES:

Δ soft plastic containers or bowls. If overheated, they begin to melt and chemicals may be released into the food. Most margarine-type containers are NOT microwave-safe.

Δ metal trimmed plates and cups. The trim causes arcing, or sparking, to occur and your microwave could be damaged.

Δ delicate china and glassware.

Δ most metal cookware. There are a few pieces of metal cookware which are designed for the microwave. Read the label before using.

Δ recycled or dyed paper products. Dyes may run, and recycled paper may contain harmful chemicals or metal bits.

FOODS THAT DO NOT COOK WELL IN THE MICROWAVE INCLUDE:

Δ puff pastry and phyllo. These need dry heat to make them crisp and flaky.

Δ angel food cakes, sponge cakes and soufflés. These also need dry heat to make them rise.

Δ eggs in the shell. They will explode.

Δ deep fat frying. Both oven and cookware manufacturers claim that this method is unsafe in the microwave. As well, correct temperatures needed for good results are difficult to maintain.

Δ yorkshire pudding and popovers. They need dry heat to make them rise.

Δ popcorn in a plain brown paper bag. The bag is likely to ignite. Use prepackaged microwave popcorn or a microwave corn popper.

Δ paraffin wax, because it contains no moisture, does not attract microwaves and therefore will not melt in the microwave oven.

Δ home canning cannot be done in the microwave.

COVERING FOOD

Δ Cover foods as you would in conventional cooking to get desired results, and to help food cook more quickly and evenly.

Δ For steamed food, cover with plastic wrap or wrap in waxed paper or parchment.

Δ To retain moisture, or to prevent splattering, cover with waxed paper or paper towelling.

MORE MICROWAVE HINTS

If your oven is a combination microwave-convection oven, be sure to wipe the inside of the oven before using on convection. This keeps microwave splatters, which are often not noticeable, from baking onto oven surfaces. You cannot use oven cleaner in your combination oven to remove these stubborn stains.

Use a ring pan to cook cakes or meat loaves in the microwave. In a regular pan, the outer edges will overcook before the center finishes cooking. Make your own ring pan by inverting a small heatproof dish in the center of the baking pan before adding food.

Check the food occasionally as it cooks. Even if the time is not up, remove it from the oven if it looks done. Your own common sense is still your best guide as to whether food is cooked or not.

Learning to cook in the microwave is like learning to walk – take one step at a time. Start with one dish before you attempt to prepare a whole microwave meal. Soon you'll wonder how you ever managed without your microwave!

MICROWAVE SHORTCUTS FOR EVERYDAY TASKS

Δ Heating milk for hot chocolate or for cooking.

Δ Melting a square of chocolate to use to decorate a cake or frost brownies or quick breads.

Δ Heating up a single serving of your favourite leftover, and not having it become crisp and stick to the pan.

Δ Softening the butter you forgot to take out of the refrigerator to make the school lunch sandwiches.

Δ Using the Delay-stand feature as a timer when your oven timer is being used for something else.

Δ Allowing you to cook many foods on the serving plate, thus making the clean-up after a meal easier and quicker.

Δ Doing a much better and faster job of cooking foods such as fish, carrot cake, and most vegetables including potatoes.

The Best of
APPETIZERS
& BEVERAGES

BAGNA CAUDA

This garlic-scented Italian "hot bath" for vegetables is the perfect way to start a casual party. Provide guests with thick slices of French bread to use as edible, drip-catching plates.

1/2 cup	butter	125 mL
1/3 cup	olive oil	75 mL
1	2-ounce (57 mL) tin flat anchovies, drained and chopped	1
1 1/2 teaspoons	finely chopped garlic	7 mL
1 cup	sour cream	250 mL
	Freshly ground pepper to taste	
	Raw vegetable sticks to dip	
1	French bread, sliced	1

1. Place butter and oil in a 4-cup (1 L) glass measure. Microwave on High for 1 minute, or until butter melts and begins to foam. Add anchovies and garlic, and microwave on High for 2 minutes, or until garlic is light brown.

2. Gradually whisk in sour cream and pepper. Microwave on Medium-low, stirring every minute, until hot but not boiling.

3. Pour into a fondue pot or chafing dish over a candle heat source. Place pot in the center of a tray of assorted raw vegetable sticks, attractively arranged. Place bread in a basket nearby and serve. Stir the mixture occasionally.

Makes 1 1/2 cups (375 mL).

TIME-SAVING TIP FOR QUICKER CLEAN-UP

If you have a microwave-safe fondue pot or appropriate casserole dish, prepare the Bagna Cauda in it for quicker clean-up.

BRIE WITH HAZELNUTS OR ALMONDS

Keep one of these small tinned Brie cheeses in your refrigerator to heat and serve to drop-in guests.

1	4-ounce (125 g) round Brie (usually purchased in a tin)	1
1/4 teaspoon	butter, melted	1 mL
1 teaspoon	finely chopped hazelnuts or almonds	5 mL
	Your favourite crackers	

1. Remove foil wrapper from cheese, being careful not to break through the outer rind.

2. Place cheese on a microwave-safe serving dish. Brush the top of the cheese with melted butter, then sprinkle with chopped nuts. Microwave on Medium-high for 45 seconds to one minute, or until the top of the cheese begins to puff. This indicates that the Brie has melted inside the rind. Watch the cheese during the last few seconds of cooking time to be sure that it does not overcook.

3. Surround the hot cheese with crackers, add a small knife and serve at once. This Brie "fondue" must be served hot, as it will harden as it cools.

Makes 4 servings.

MICROWAVE HINT – GETTING THE BEST FLAVOUR FROM CHEESE

To bring out the flavour of most cheeses, warm them in the microwave for a few seconds just before serving; using Medium power. Check often, and be careful not to overheat, or the cheese will melt, then toughen.

CAPONATA

Best made in the summer when tomatoes are tastiest, but drained, canned Italian-style plum tomatoes substitute nicely for the fresh ones. Who can resist a plump, shiny, purple eggplant any season?

1 pound	eggplant, peeled, cut into 1/2 inch (1 cm) cubes	500 g
	Salt	
2 tablespoons	olive oil	25 mL
1 cup	chopped celery	250 mL
1/3 cup	chopped onion	75 mL
3 tablespoons	red wine vinegar	50 mL
2 teaspoons	sugar	10 mL
1 1/2 cups	seeded, chopped tomatoes	375 mL
1 tablespoon	tomato paste	15 mL
2 tablespoons	chopped green olives	25 mL
1 tablespoon	capers	15 mL
2	anchovy fillets, rinsed and chopped	2
	Freshly ground pepper	
1 tablespoon	pine nuts	15 mL

1. Place eggplant in a colander in the sink and sprinkle with salt. Leave for 30 minutes, then rinse cubes and pat dry.

2. In a large microwave-safe casserole mix eggplant, oil, celery and onion. Microwave on High for 8 to 10 minutes, or until vegetables are tender. Stir occasionally.

3. Stir in all remaining ingredients except pine nuts. Microwave on High for 10 minutes, stirring several times. Taste and add more pepper, vinegar or salt if needed. Stir in pine nuts.

4. Refrigerate until cold. Serve with French bread and cold butter.

Makes 4 cups (1 L).

HELPFUL HINT – SAVING LEFTOVER TOMATO PASTE

Leftover tomato paste – drop by tablespoonfuls onto waxed paper on a plate and freeze until firm. Place in a freezer bag and label before freezing. Defrost in the microwave as needed.

HONEY GARLIC WINGS

This is a microwave version of a recipe that my mother, Dorothy Searles, has made for years – always to rave reviews. Her wings take over an hour to cook; mine take 10 minutes after marinating, and are almost as good as Mom's!

2 1/2 – 3 pounds	chicken wings	1.25 to 1.5 kg
1 cup	dark brown sugar	250 mL
1 teaspoon	garlic salt	5 mL
1/2 cup	soy sauce	125 mL
1/4 cup	liquid honey	50 mL
1/4 cup	water	50 mL
2 teaspoons	cornstarch	10 mL

1. Cut the wings into 3 pieces at the joints. Discard tips, or save for making stock.

2. Place the remaining wing pieces in a large bowl.

3. Combine brown sugar, garlic salt, soy sauce, honey, water and cornstarch in a 4-cup (1 L) glass measure and stir until sugar dissolves. Microwave on High for 3 1/2 minutes, stirring after 2 minutes, until marinade boils and thickens slightly. Pour over wings, stir to coat, cover and refrigerate for 2 to 3 hours or overnight.

4. Arrange the wing pieces in a spoke pattern in a large heatproof dish with the meatiest part of the pieces facing the outer edge of the plate. Pour enough marinade over the wings to coat the bottom of the pan. Brush chicken pieces with sauce.

5. Cover with waxed paper and microwave on High for 8 to 10 minutes. Turn wings over halfway through cooking. Wings should be tender and brown. Repeat procedure with any remaining pieces, until all pieces are cooked.

6. The wings can be cooked early in the day, refrigerated with the marinade and reheated in the microwave at serving time. Reheat in the marinade, which becomes a lovely, thick sauce.

Makes 10 to 12 appetizer servings.

MICROWAVE HINT - TO SOFTEN HARD BROWN SUGAR

Place 1 cup of sugar in a bowl with a slice of fresh bread. Cover and microwave on High for 1/2 to 1 minute, or until soft.

Hot Crab Dip

This is the perfect nibble to prepare at the last minute, as all of the ingredients store well for a long time. Keep them on hand for unexpected company.

2 teaspoons	sliced almonds	10 mL
8 ounces	cream cheese, softened	250 g
l tablespoon	sour cream	15 mL
2 teaspoons	lemon juice	10 mL
	Hot pepper sauce to taste	
l	4-ounce (114 mL) tin crabmeat, drained and flaked	1
	Crackers or celery sticks to dip	

l. Place the almonds in a small, heatproof bowl. Microwave on High for 3 minutes or until toasted. Check and stir during cooking.

2. Combine the cheese with sour cream, lemon juice and hot pepper sauce, and mix well. Stir in crabmeat; taste and adjust seasonings.

3. Microwave on Medium for 3 to 5 minutes, or until heated through. Pour hot mixture into a serving crock and sprinkle with toasted almonds. Surround with crackers or celery and serve at once.

Makes l 1/2 cups (375 mL).

Regular Oven Method – Hot Crab Dip

Place crab mixture in oven-proof crock. Heat at 350° F (180° C) for 20 to 30 minutes, or until heated through. Sprinkle with toasted almonds before serving.

Microwave Hint - to Soften Cream Cheese

Remove foil, place cheese on a plate and microwave on Low for 2 minutes, or until soft.

MARINATED MUSHROOMS

Fill a cork-top glass bottle with these tasty morsels for a personalized gift. Be sure to tell recipient to store them in the refrigerator.

1/2 cup	red wine vinegar	125 mL
1/4 cup	water	50 mL
2 tablespoons	olive oil	25 mL
5	black peppercorns	5
1	small bay leaf	1
2	whole cloves	2
1	clove garlic, peeled and halved	1
1/2 teaspoon	salt	2 mL
8 ounces	small fresh mushrooms, cleaned	250 g

1. Combine all ingredients except mushrooms in an 8-cup (2 L) microwave-safe casserole. Microwave on High for 2 minutes or until boiling. Add mushrooms, cover casserole and microwave on High for 5 minutes, stirring occasionally.

2. Cool. Remove bay leaf. Spoon mushrooms and liquid into a jar large enough to hold them. Cover top with plastic wrap and secure with a tight fitting lid.

3. Store Marinated Mushrooms in the refrigerator for 1 week before serving. Mushrooms must be refrigerated.

Makes 1 pint (500 mL).

MICROWAVE GIFT SUGGESTION

Give a new microwave owner a large (8 to 10-cup) (2 to 2.5 L) glass measuring cup. This is one of the handiest and most used items in my kitchen. With this measuring cup, you can measure and cook in the same dish, watch the food as it cooks to determine doneness, and pour foods easily into serving dishes.

MICROWAVE HINT-FROZEN HORS D'OEUVRES HEATED IN MINUTES

Defrost frozen pastries in the microwave, then crisp them in a 425° F (220° C) oven for 2 to 5 minutes before serving.

MEXICAN BEAN DIP

I first prepared this dip in a 90-second snack segment on the children's TV show, "Take Part." The kids and crew loved it.

1	tin refried beans	1
1/2 cup	cream cheese, softened	125 mL
1/2 to 1 teaspoon	chili powder	2 to 5 mL
1/4 teaspoon	garlic salt	1 mL
	Salt to taste	
	Celery sticks,	
	green or red pepper slices,	
	cucumber slices	
	Corn chips	

1. Mix beans, cheese and spices in a large microwave-safe bowl. Stir to mix well. Microwave on High 2 to 3 minutes, or until hot. Stir once during cooking. Taste and adjust seasonings.

2. Spoon into a serving bowl and surround with vegetable sticks and corn chips to dip.

Makes 6 to 8 servings.

WHEN KIDS COOK MICROWAVE:

Δ show them how all of the controls work.

Δ stress that the microwave must never be operated empty.

Δ show them which dishes can be used in the microwave.

Δ show them how to arrange food so that it cooks evenly.

Δ tell them to use oven mitts to remove dishes from the oven.

Δ mention that food holds heat, so let it stand before eating.

Δ let it be known that clean-up is part of cooking!

MICROWAVE SNACK – POPCORN AND CHIPS

Popcorn tastes better hot, so warm it up in a large microwave-safe bowl on High power until heated through. This works for potato chips too.

QUICK NACHOS

Cover a paper plate with tortilla chips. Sprinkle with grated cheddar cheese and taco sauce. Microwave on High just until cheese melts; time needed depends on quantity.

Regular Oven Method - SMOKED SALMON CHEESECAKE

Pour filling (do not heat) into a 9-inch (22 cm) springform pan sprinkled with the crumb mixture. Bake at 325° F (160° C) for 1 hour and 10 minutes, or until the cheesecake is almost set at the center. Turn off oven and leave cheesecake in oven for 1 hour more. Cool to room temperature before wrapping and refrigerating.

MICROWAVE HINT - TO DRY HERBS

This is a great way to save the parsley left over from the huge bunch that you had to buy when you needed 2 sprigs! Place 1/2 cup fresh herbs on a paper towel on a paper plate. Cover with another paper towel. Microwave on High 2 to 3 minutes, or until just crisp. Check often during cooking and do not overcook. Do not use the same plate and towels for 2 successive batches, as the towels, when overheated, may ignite.

SMOKED SALMON CHEESECAKE

As an hors d'oeuvre or a light luncheon entrée, this cheesecake is sensational. Make 2 days ahead to let it "mellow." It is very easy to make, in spite of the long list of ingredients!

1 teaspoon	butter	5 mL
2 tablespoons	dry breadcrumbs	25 mL
1 tablespoon	grated gruyère cheese	15 mL
1 teaspoon	minced fresh dillweed	5 mL
1 tablespoon	butter	15 mL
1/2 cup	chopped onion	125 mL
2 8-oz (250 g)	packages cream cheese, softened	
3	medium eggs	3
1/3 cup	grated gruyère cheese	75 mL
1/4 cup	light cream	50 mL
1/4 teaspoon	salt	1 mL
6 ounces	smoked salmon, chopped	190 g
3 tablespoons	snipped fresh dillweed	50 mL
	Sour cream and dill sprigs to garnish	

1. Butter the bottom and sides of a 9-inch (22 cm) round glass cake pan. Place a circle of buttered waxed paper, cut to fit the bottom of the pan, in the pan if you plan to remove the cheesecake from the pan for serving.

2. Combine the first 4 ingredients and sprinkle in the pan, coating the bottom and sides with the mixture. Set aside.

3. Place 1 tablespoon (15 mL) butter and the onion in a 2-cup (500 mL) glass measure and microwave on High for 1 1/2 to 2 minutes, or until onion is soft.

4. Place onion mixture, cheese, eggs, 1/3 cup (75 mL) gruyère, cream and salt in food processor and process until smooth. Add salmon and dill, and process until just mixed. The salmon should still be in small chunks in the mixture.

5. Pour mixture into a large glass bowl and microwave on Medium for 4 minutes, or until hot. Stir twice. Pour hot filling into prepared pan. Microwave on Medium for 8 to 10 minutes, or until mixture is almost set. It will finish setting as it cools.

6. Cool to room temperature, then wrap and refrigerate at least 1 day before serving. Garnish with sour cream piped onto the top, and sprigs of fresh dillweed.

Makes 8 servings.

SMOOTH LIVER PÂTÉ

A liver pâté that freezes without becoming crumbly. The butter is the reason for this, and for the creamy smooth texture.

l pound	chicken livers, chopped	500 g
l	large onion, chopped	1
l	clove garlic, a large one, cut in half	1
l teaspoon	fresh thyme leaves (1/4 tsp. dried)	5 mL
3/4 cup	water	175 mL
1/2 teaspoon	salt	2 mL
l	bay leaf	1
1 1/2 cups	soft butter	375 mL
l tablespoon	brandy	15 mL
l teaspoon	coarsely cracked pepper	5 mL

ASPIC FOR 1 SMALL PÂTÉ

1/3 cup	reserved cooking liquid or chicken stock	75 mL
l teaspoon	unflavoured gelatin	5 mL

1. Place liver, onion, garlic, thyme, water, salt and bay leaf in a microwave-safe casserole. Cover and microwave on High for 4 minutes, or until very hot. Stir, then cover and microwave on Medium for 4 to 6 minutes, or until liver is fully cooked. Stir once during cooking.

2. Use a slotted spoon to transfer solids to a food processor. Process until smooth. (Strain and reserve cooking liquid to make aspic, if desired. Strain through a coffee filter for crystal-clear aspic.)

3. With food processor running, add butter a bit at a time along with brandy and pepper, and continue to process until well blended. Taste and adjust seasonings.

4. Pour pâté mixture into one large or several small crocks and cool to room temperature before wrapping and freezing.

Thyme

5. If the pâté is to be served the next day, it may be decorated with aspic. Decorate the top with bits of red and green pepper, parsley, dillweed or whole peppercorns of various colours before topping with aspic.

To Make Aspic:

1. Place stock or reserved cooking liquid in a 1-cup (250 mL) glass measure and sprinkle gelatin over. Let stand 5 minutes. Microwave on Low for 1 minute, or until gelatin dissolves. Stir once.

2. Cool until aspic begins to thicken, then spoon a thin layer carefully over the decorated pâté.

3. Once the first aspic layer solidifies (place in the refrigerator to speed up this process), add a second thin layer of aspic to completely cover the decorations. Chill until aspic is firm, then wrap and refrigerate until ready to use. This pâté will keep for several days.

Makes 1 large or 5 small pâtés, about 6 servings each for the small ones.

Gelatin in the Microwave

Soften gelatin for 5 minutes at room temperature, then dissolve in the microwave using Low power. Time needed depends on amount. Stir occasionally.

ANTIPASTO

Takes a while to prepare but makes a large batch and it freezes well. Freeze in small containers and defrost in the microwave as needed.

2	carrots, peeled and thinly sliced	2
1/2 cup	chopped green pepper	125 mL
1/3 cup	chopped sweet red pepper	75 mL
1/2 cup	chopped celery	125 mL
1/2 cup	tiny cauliflowerets	125 mL
1/2 cup	chopped pitted black olives	125 mL
1/2 cup	sliced mushrooms	125 mL
1/2 cup	small white pickled onions	125 mL
1 cup	chopped sweet pickles	250 mL
1/2 cup	chopped stuffed olives	125 mL
1	7 1/2 oz (213 g) tin tomato sauce	1
2/3 cup	ketchup	150 mL
1 tablespoon	olive oil	15 mL
1	tin water-packed solid tuna, drained and flaked	1

1. Place all ingredients except tuna in a large casserole or microwave simmer pot. Stir to mix. Cover and microwave on High for 5 minutes, or until boiling. Stir once.

2. Microwave on Medium-low for 15 to 20 minutes, or until carrots are crisp-tender. Stir every 5 minutes.

3. Add tuna to the cooked vegetable mixture. Refrigerate for 2 weeks, or freeze for up to 3 months.

4. Serve with crackers or French bread and cold butter.

Makes 5 cups (1.25 L)

MICROWAVE HINT – PLASTIC CONTAINERS

If you freeze or refrigerate food in plastic containers, transfer food to a microwave-safe container before defrosting or heating in the microwave. Unless a plastic container has "microwave-safe" printed on it, do not use it in the microwave.

UNPLEASANT ODOUR IN YOUR MICROWAVE ?

Place a slice of lemon or a bit of vinegar in a 1-cup (250mL) measure full of water. Microwave on High for 2 minutes, or until boiling. Leave in the oven for 5 minutes, then remove and wipe the inside of the oven to dry it.

CHOCOLATE COFFEE

A rich way to end a meal – have this instead of dessert.

1 cup	strong coffee	250mL
	Milk or light cream to taste	
1 ounce	crème de cacao	28.5mL
	Sweetened whipped cream	
	Cocoa powder	

1. Combine coffee and milk in a microwave-safe mug. Microwave on Medium for 1 to 2 minutes or until very hot but not boiling. Stir in crème de cacao.

2. Top with a generous dollop of sweetened whipped cream and a dusting of cocoa.

Variation: Add cinnamon to taste, or serve with a cinnamon stick to stir.

Makes 1 serving.

MICROWAVE HOT CHOCOLATE

Probably one of the first things you'll prepare in your new microwave. Fill a microwave-safe mug with milk. Microwave on Medium for 2 minutes, or until hot. Stir in your favourite chocolate drink powder or syrup, to taste. If desired, add a marshmallow and microwave on Medium for 30 seconds more, until marshmallow puffs up.

Makes 1 serving.

MICROWAVE HINT - LEFTOVER COFFEE

Store leftover coffee in a covered container in the refrigerator to reheat in your microwave and enjoy later in the day.

HOT CHOCOLATE MIX

This dry mix is a terrific Christmas gift for children to prepare. Spoon it into an attractive canister or mug for gift giving, or take it along on camping trips for a quick campfire treat.

2 cups	instant powdered skim milk	500 mL
3/4 cup	sugar	175 mL
l/2 cup	unsweetened cocoa	125 mL
	Dash of salt	

1. Measure milk powder, sugar , cocoa and salt into a large bowl.

2. Stir to mix well. Place a sieve over another large bowl. Pour mixture into sieve and stir through into lower bowl.

3. Pour mixture into a large jar.

4. To package for gift giving: decorate a paper cup or glass jar with stickers or drawings. Fill with chocolate mixture. Cover with jar lid or plastic wrap and an elastic band. Decorate with a ribbon and write these directions on a card and attach to the package:

> *"Microwave l mugful of water or milk to just below boiling. (Milk: Medium for 2 minutes. Water: High for l l/2 minutes.) Add 2 tablespoons Hot Chocolate Mix and stir until well mixed."*

Makes 2 3/4 cups (675 mL) of mix.

MICROWAVE HINT

Be sure that the mugs you are using have no metallic trim. This trim will cause arcing in the microwave.

HOT LEMONADE

This drink is a wonderful tonic for that shivery, fragile way that you feel when you're coming down with a cold.

1/4 cup	lemon juice	50 mL
3/4 cup	boiling water	175 mL
1 tablespoon	honey, or to taste	15 mL
1	cinnamon stick, 2 inches (5 cm) long	1
1	thin slice lemon	1
	Grated nutmeg	
1 ounce	whiskey or brandy (optional)	28.5 mL

1. Combine lemon juice, water, honey and cinnamon stick in a microwave-safe mug and stir until honey dissolves. Microwave on High for 1 to 2 minutes or until very hot.

2. Top with lemon slice and a sprinkling of nutmeg. Stir in whiskey or brandy for the adult version.

Makes 1 serving.

HOT TOMATO SIPPER

A savoury start to a winter meal, or a healthy between-meal snack when you leave out the vodka!

1 cup	tomato juice or vegetable cocktail	250 mL
	Dash of garlic salt and basil	
	Salt and freshly ground pepper to taste	
	Tabasco sauce to taste	
1 ounce	vodka (optional)	28.5 mL
1	thin slice of lemon	1
1	celery stick	1

1. Place all ingredients except vodka, lemon and celery in a heat-proof mug. Microwave on High for 1 to 2 minutes, or until very hot.

2. Stir in vodka. Garnish with lemon and celery and serve hot.

Variation: Omit vodka and add a dash of Worcestershire sauce. Heat as above.

Makes 1 serving.

TO TEST IF A DISH IS MICROWAVE-SAFE

Place the dish to be tested in the microwave with a glass measuring cup containing one cup of water. Microwave on High for 1 minute, or until the water is hot. If the dish is still cool, it is safe for microwave use. If the dish becomes hot, it should not be used for microwave cooking.

SPICED CIDER

A fancy jar of cheesecloth-wrapped spice bundles and a bottle of fresh apple cider makes a lovely hostess or holiday gift. Be sure to include recipe with your gift.

l cup	fresh apple cider or juice	250 mL
l	cinnamon stick, 2 inches (5 cm) long	1
2	whole cloves	2
2	whole allspice berries	2
l ounce	brandy (optional)	28.5 mL
	Freshly grated nutmeg	

1. Pour cider into a microwave-safe mug. Put cinnamon stick in mug. Tie the cloves and allspice in a small piece of cheesecloth and add to cider. Microwave on High for 2 minutes, or until hot.

2. Remove the spice bundle and stir in brandy if desired. Sprinkle with nutmeg and serve hot.

Makes l serving.

MICROWAVE LUNCH ON THE RUN

Heat a mug of soup in the microwave, then take it back to your desk with you, along with your favourite cheese and meat on a bun, melted to perfection in the microwave.

The Best of

BREAKFAST, BRUNCH, BREADS & BREAKFAST PRESERVES

ASPARAGUS CHEESE OMELETTE

This delicious puffy omelette will please the eye as well as the palate. As with all egg dishes, be sure to use Medium power or lower so that the protein in the egg remains tender.

1 cup	chopped fresh asparagus	250 mL
4 teaspoons	butter, divided	20 mL
3	eggs, separated	3
1 tablespoon	water	15 mL
	Salt and pepper to taste	
1/2 cup	shredded cheese, mozzarella, cheddar, Swiss or your favourite	125 mL
	Paprika	

1. Place asparagus and 1 teaspoon (5 mL) butter in a small microwave-safe bowl. Cover with plastic wrap and microwave on High for 2 minutes, or until asparagus is crisp-tender. Cover and keep warm.

2. Beat egg whites until they form soft peaks. Whisk yolks and water together, then fold gently into beaten whites.

3. Melt remaining 3 teaspoons (15 mL) butter in a 9-inch (22 cm) microwave-safe pie plate. Tilt pan to coat bottom with butter. Microwave on High for 1 1/2 minutes, or until bubbly.

4. Gently spoon egg mixture into pie plate and spread evenly with a spatula or knife. Microwave on Medium for 3 to 4 minutes, or until eggs are set.

5. Sprinkle cheese over the whole omelette. Sprinkle lightly with salt and pepper and spoon hot asparagus onto one half of the omelette. (If the asparagus has cooled, reheat in the microwave on High for about 30 seconds.) Fold omelette in half to cover asparagus, and sprinkle the top lightly with paprika. Cut into two pieces and serve at once, with Fresh Tomato Salsa (recipe on page 89).

Makes 2 servings.

MICROWAVE OMELETTE VARIATIONS

Fill your omelette with lightly steamed fresh vegetables such asparagus, mushrooms or green peppers and a few gratings of your favourite cheese. For an interesting change, try stuffing your omelette with cooked shrimp, chopped cooked artichoke hearts, thinly sliced cooked spicy Italian sausage or chopped smoked salmon sautéed with butter and shallots. Accompany with a dollop of cold, spicy Fresh Tomato Salsa and a warm whole wheat roll.

MICROWAVE HINT – OMELETTES

Make your omelette in a browning dish so that the outside will be brown when you fold the omelette in half. Preheat the browning dish before cooking omelette.

Regular Oven Method
BAKED PANCAKE

Melt butter in pan in hot oven and stir in brown sugar and syrup. Pour batter in as above, and bake in a preheated 375° F (190° C) oven for 20 minutes, or until top springs back when touched. Invert as at right.

MICROWAVE MAPLE BREAKFAST TREATS

Stir maple syrup into your microwave oatmeal for a yummy Canadian winter treat. Warm maple syrup in a microwave-safe jug before serving with pancakes, waffles or French toast. It only takes a few seconds on High to reach the desired temperature, so watch that it doesn't overheat.

BAKED PANCAKE

An easy way to prepare pancakes for the whole family at the same time.

1/4 cup	butter or margarine	50 mL
1/4 cup	brown sugar	50 mL
1/3 cup	maple or pancake syrup	75 mL
1	egg	1
1 cup	milk	250 mL
1 tablespoon	vegetable oil	15 mL
1 1/4 cups	all-purpose flour	300 mL
2 tablespoons	sugar	25 mL
2 teaspoons	baking powder	10 mL
1/2 teaspoon	salt	2 mL

1. Place butter, brown sugar and syrup in an 8-inch (20 cm) round glass baking pan. Microwave on High for 1 minute, or until butter is melted. Stir to mix butter and sugar and to coat the bottom of the pan with the mixture.

2. In a large bowl, mix together the egg, milk and oil. In another bowl combine the flour, sugar, baking powder and salt.

3. Add the dry mixture to the egg mixture and stir with a spoon or whisk until the batter is very smooth.

4. Carefully spoon the pancake batter over the syrup mixture in the pan. Microwave on Medium for 10 minutes, or until a toothpick inserted into the center of the pancake comes out clean. Cover with waxed paper and let stand 5 minutes before serving.

5. Carefully invert the pancake in one quick motion onto a serving plate large enough to hold both the pancake and the syrup topping which forms in the pan. Cut into wedges and serve hot.

Makes 4 to 6 servings.

Cheese Soufflé with Microwave Help

A soufflé must be baked in a hot oven since it needs dry heat to make it rise. However, you can do several of the preparation steps in the microwave to get your soufflé into the oven faster.

	Butter and grated Parmesan cheese	
3 tablespoons	butter	50 mL
3 tablespoons	flour	50 mL
1/2 teaspoon	salt	2 mL
	Dash of pepper	
1/4 teaspoon	dry mustard	1 mL
1 cup	milk	250 mL
4	eggs, separated	4
1 cup	grated sharp cheddar cheese	250 mL

1. Preheat regular oven to 400° F (200° C).

2. Butter a 6-cup (1.5 L) soufflé dish, then sprinkle in enough grated Parmesan to coat bottom and sides with cheese. Set aside.

3. Place 3 tablespoons (50 mL) butter in an 8-cup (2 L) glass measure or bowl. Microwave on High for 30 seconds or until melted. Whisk in flour and seasonings all at once. Gradually whisk in milk. Microwave on Medium for 3 to 5 minutes, whisking every 2 minutes, until sauce is hot and thickened.

4. While sauce cooks, whip egg whites until stiff but not dry.

5. Add cheese to sauce and stir until it melts. Beat egg yolks in a small bowl, then whisk them into the cheese sauce.

6. Stir 1 tablespoon (15 mL) of the beaten whites into the cheese sauce, then carefully fold the remaining whites into the sauce.

7. Spoon the mixture into the prepared soufflé dish.

8. Place the soufflé in the preheated oven and immediately reduce oven temperature to 375° F (190° C). Bake for 30 to 35 minutes, or until soufflé is puffed and golden brown. Serve at once – a soufflé waits for no one!

Makes 4 servings.

Microwave Hint – Whisks

Always use a whisk to stir microwave cream sauces – the sauce will be smoother as a result.

Parsley

EGG IN A HAM CUP

Everyone from a 4-year-old to a senior can make this quick, easy meal. When it first appeared in my *Ottawa Citizen* column, it was part of a Mother's Day surprise breakfast menu for children to prepare. I have since demonstrated it to a seniors' club and they enjoyed it just as much.

For each serving:

1	thin slice of ham	1
1	egg	1
	Pepper	
1/2 teaspoon	grated cheddar or Parmesan cheese (optional)	2 mL
	Paprika (optional)	
	Fresh parsley sprig	

1. Press ham slice into a small heatproof bowl so that it forms a cup. Microwave on High for 15 to 20 seconds to warm up the ham.

2. Break egg into the ham "cup" and sprinkle lightly with pepper. Pierce yolk and white of the egg carefully several times. Cover dish with microwave-safe plastic wrap. Microwave on Medium for 1 to 1 1/2 minutes or until the egg white appears to be almost set.

3. Sprinkle cheese over the egg. Let stand 1 minute before serving.

4. Transfer the ham and egg to a plate. If you are making more than one serving, keep warm in a 200° F (100° C) oven while you cook the remaining servings in the microwave. Be sure to remove plastic wrap if you are placing the plates in a hot oven.

5. To serve (once the cheese has melted), sprinkle the egg with paprika and garnish with a sprig of parsley. Serve hot with warm English muffins or toast.

Makes 1 serving.

MICROWAVE HINT - OATMEAL FOR ONE

Combine 3/4 cup (175 mL) water and 1/3 cup (75 mL) oatmeal in a microwave-safe cereal bowl. Microwave on High for 2 minutes, or until oatmeal bubbles. Let stand for 2 minutes, then stir before serving.

EGGS BENEDICT

Once you have mastered the Microwave Hollandaise Sauce, use it to enhance the flavor of steamed broccoli or asparagus.

4	eggs
4	slices cooked ham or back bacon
2	English muffins, split and toasted
	Microwave Hollandaise Sauce (recipe follows)
	Parsley sprigs and cherry tomatoes to garnish

1. To poach an egg in the microwave: Measure 1/4 cup (50 mL) water and a few drops vinegar into a small, flat-bottomed microwave-safe dish. Microwave on High until the water boils.

2. Break an egg into the boiling water. Pierce yolk and white several times with a fork or toothpick. Cover with plastic wrap and microwave on Medium for 45 seconds to 1 minute, or until egg is almost cooked.

3. Keep warm in a 200° F (100° C) oven until needed. Repeat procedure with remaining eggs.

4. Toast muffins and heat ham or bacon in microwave on High until hot. Place meat on muffin. Top with poached egg. Pour warm Microwave Hollandaise Sauce over egg and garnish. Serve at once.

Makes 4 servings.

MICROWAVE EGG COOKERY

Prick both yolk and white before poaching eggs in the microwave. Never cook an egg in the shell in the microwave – it will definitely explode!

Use Medium power or lower for good results, and to prevent "explosions."

Overcooking will also cause this result.

Since microwaves are attracted to fat, the yolk will cook more quickly than the white. For a soft yolk, remove the egg from the microwave when the white is not quite set. Cover and let stand for 1 to 2 minutes to finish cooking white.

MICROWAVE HOLLANDAISE SAUCE

4	egg yolks	4
1/2 cup	whipping cream	125 mL
1/4 teaspoon	salt	1 mL
	Pinch of dry mustard	
2 tablespoons	lemon juice	25 mL
1/2 cup	butter	125 mL

1. Combine egg yolks, cream, salt, mustard and lemon juice in a 4-cup (1 L) glass measure.

2. Melt butter in a microwave-safe bowl on High for 1 minute or until melted.

3. Whisk butter into yolk mixture until smooth. Microwave on Medium for 3 minutes, stirring every 30 seconds until sauce thickens.

Refrigerate leftover sauce; reheat using Low power and whisking often.

Makes 1 cup (250 mL) of sauce.

EASY HOLLANDAISE SAUCE

This version takes the guesswork out of Hollandaise. It's perfect to carry to the cottage for that very special lakeside brunch.

3/4 cup	mayonnaise	175 mL
1/4 cup	sour cream	50 mL
1 tablespoon	lemon juice	15 mL
2 teaspoons	prepared mustard	10 mL

Combine ingredients in a glass bowl or measure. Microwave on Medium for 1 to 2 minutes, or until very hot. Stir every 30 seconds. Can be prepared ahead, refrigerated and warmed up at serving time.

Makes about 1 cup (250 mL)

MICROWAVE HINT

Breakfast pastries and sweet rolls can be defrosted and reheated in the microwave. Very little time is required to perform these tasks. Keep in mind that sugary or buttery filling can become very hot, even if the outside of the pastry seems cool, so allow the pastry to stand for a few minutes before serving.

Ham and Asparagus Rolls

Asparagus is available for most of the year now, so this recipe is no longer just a springtime treat.

1 pound	crisply cooked asparagus spears	500 g
4	thin slices good smoked ham	4
2 tablespoons	butter	25 mL
2 tablespoons	flour	25 mL
1/4 teaspoon	dry mustard	1 mL
1/2 teaspoon	salt	2 mL
	Freshly ground pepper	
1 cup	milk	250 mL
3/4 cup	grated Swiss or sharp cheddar cheese	175 mL
	Paprika	

1. Divide asparagus into 4 equal portions. Roll each portion in a ham slice and place each ham roll on a separate microwave-safe dish or luncheon plate.

2. To make sauce: Melt butter in a 4-cup (1 L) glass measure on High for 30 seconds. Stir in flour, mustard, salt and pepper all at once. Slowly whisk in milk. Microwave on Medium for 3 to 5 minutes, or until thickened. Whisk twice during cooking.

3. Add cheese and paprika to sauce and stir until cheese melts. Taste and adjust seasonings.

4. Pour 1/4 of the sauce over each ham roll. Sprinkle lightly with paprika. Microwave each serving on High for 30 seconds to 1 minute, or until heated through.

Makes 4 servings.

Regular Oven Method – Ham and Asparagus Rolls

Make sauce in a pot on the stovetop or in a double boiler, stirring constantly until thickened. Put ham rolls in oven-proof dish or dishes and bake at 425° F (220° C) for 10 minutes, or until hot and bubbling.

Makes 4 servings.

Microwave Hint – Smooth Sauces

Stirring sauces often with a whisk during cooking will help prevent curdling, lumpiness and boiling over.

BOSTON BROWN BREAD

Serve this steamy bread with seafood chowder for a warming winter supper.

l cup	buttermilk	250 mL
1/3 cup	molasses	75 mL
1/2 teaspoon	baking powder	2 mL
1/2 teaspoon	baking soda	2 mL
1/2 teaspoon	salt	2 mL
1/2 cup	all-purpose flour	125 mL
1/2 cup	whole wheat flour	125 mL
1/2 cup	cornmeal	125 mL
1/2 cup	raisins	125 mL

1. Combine all ingredients and mix well.

2. Pour batter into a lightly greased 4 or 6-cup (1 to 1.5 L) casserole or microwave-safe bowl. (I use a 6-cup (1.5 L) soufflé dish to get a nice round loaf.) Cover tightly with microwave-safe plastic wrap. Microwave on Medium for 9 to l0 minutes, or until bread tests done with a toothpick.

3. Let stand, covered for l0 minutes then uncovered for 5 minutes more. Serve warm.

Makes l loaf.

COOKING TIP – BUTTERMILK POWDER

In the past, I often rejected a recipe that called for a small amount of buttermilk because I didn't want to buy a whole quart. (Why isn't buttermilk sold in smaller pints or half pints (500 or 250 mL cartons)? In cooking, I often use buttermilk powder purchased in a bulk food store. Mix 4 to 8 tablespoons (50 to 125 mL) of the powder with enough water to make a cup (250 mL). It can be used immediately in cooking, but should stand in the refrigerator for 8 hours before drinking.

OLD FASHIONED MASHED POTATO ROLLS

I tried for many years to duplicate the flavour of cloverleaf rolls made by my friend Martha Blanchette's mother, and this recipe comes very close. Though the final baking is done in a regular oven, doing the preparation steps in the microwave saves time without sacrificing anything.

l	large potato (to make 1/2 cup (125 mL) mashed)	1
1 1/4 cups	milk	300 mL
1/2 cup	shortening	125 mL
4 to 4 1/2 cups	all-purpose flour	l L to 1.125 L
2 teaspoons	instant or rapid yeast	10 mL
1/3 cup	sugar	5 mL
l teaspoon	salt	5 mL
l	egg, lightly beaten	1

1. Wash potato and prick skin several times. Microwave on High for 4 to 6 minutes, or until potato is soft. Cut in half, scoop out pulp, and mash.

2. Measure 1/2 cup (125 mL) mashed potatoes into a large glass measuring cup. Add milk and shortening to potatoes. Microwave on High for 2 minutes, or until mixture is heated to 125° to 130° F (45° to 50° C). Use a temperature probe for this if you wish. The shortening may not be completely melted when the desired temperature is reached. Stir briefly and it will finish melting.

3. Combine 3 1/2 cups (825 mL) flour, yeast, sugar and salt in a large mixing bowl. Stir in milk mixture and egg.

4. Add enough of the remaining flour to make the mixture easy to handle. Knead on a lightly floured board for 8 to 10 minutes, or until smooth.

5. Cover with a clean tea towel and let rest for 10 minutes.

6. Butter 2 muffin pans. Place 3 small balls of dough in each section of pans (like cloverleaf rolls). Cover pans with a tea towel and let rise in a warm place for 45 minutes to l hour, or until rolls have doubled in size.

7. Bake in a preheated 400° F (200° C) oven for l0 to 12 minutes, or until golden brown. Serve warm.

Makes 2 dozen.

BASKETS IN THE MICROWAVE

For short cooking times, you can use wicker baskets, wooden bowls or paper plates in the microwave.

MICROWAVE SAFE LIDS

Some microwave-safe dishes and bowls are sold with storage lids that are not microwave-safe. Do not use these lids in the microwave unless you are sure that it is safe to do so.

Proofing Yeast Bread Dough

You can cut the time required for bread to rise in half by proofing the dough in your microwave. Though it is possible to bake bread in a microwave, I think that a conventional oven produces a better looking and tasting loaf. Follow these steps, using your favorite bread recipe:

(Yield: 2 loaves)

1. First rising: shape the kneaded dough into a smooth ball and place in a well-greased, large microwave-safe bowl. Brush top with oil. Cover loosely with plastic wrap. Put 3 cups (750 mL) of water in a square baking dish and place the bowl of dough in the dish. Microwave on Warm (10% power) for 25 to 30 minutes, or until dough doubles in bulk.

2. Second rising: punch the dough down and shape into loaves. Place in well-greased glass or ceramic loaf pans and repeat the above proofing procedure. This proofing technique can also be used for yeast rolls; however, unless you have microwave muffin pans, you will have to make pan rolls in a 9-inch (1.5 L) round glass baking dish.

Microwave Hint – Defrosting Frozen Bread Dough

Place 1 loaf of dough in a lightly oiled microwave-safe loaf pan and cover pan tightly with microwave-safe plastic wrap. Set loaf pan in a larger pan containing 3 cups (750 mL) of boiling water. Microwave on Warm (lowest power level) for 5 minutes, then let stand for 10 to 15 minutes in pan of water, or until completely defrosted. For bread, proof as explained above. Dough can also be used for pizza crust, rolls or focaccia.

PUMPKIN MUFFINS

Chop up the Halloween pumpkin and cook it in the microwave to make these spicy, moist muffins. Freeze leftover cooked pumpkin in small containers for easy defrosting.

1 cup	flour	250 mL
2 tablespoons	wheat germ	25 mL
1 teaspoon	baking powder	5 mL
1/4 teaspoon	salt	1 mL
1/2 teaspoon	cinnamon	2 mL
1/4 teaspoon	nutmeg	1 mL
1/4 teaspoon	ginger	1 mL
1/8 teaspoon	cloves	0.5 mL
1/3 cup	lightly packed brown sugar	75 mL
1	egg	1
1/3 cup	milk	75 mL
1/2 cup	cooked, puréed pumpkin	125 mL
2 tablespoons	oil	25 mL
1/2 cup	chopped nuts or raisins (optional)	125 mL

1. In a large bowl combine flour, wheat germ, baking powder, salt, spices and brown sugar.

2. In a smaller bowl beat together egg, milk, pumpkin and oil. Stir this mixture into the dry mixture along with raisins or nuts if desired. Stir just enough to combine ingredients.

3. Spoon batter into a paper-lined microwave muffin pan or small heatproof dishes. Fill 2/3 full. Microwave 6 muffins at a time on High for 4 1/2 to 6 minutes or until muffins test done with a toothpick. Repeat with remaining batter. Three muffins will take 3 to 4 minutes to cook. Let stand for 5 minutes before serving.

Makes about 10 muffins.

MICROWAVE HINT FOR MUFFINS AND CUPCAKES

To improve the colour of finished muffins, dip them in a mixture of 1/4 cup (50 mL) brown sugar and 1/2 teaspoon (2 mL) cinnamon. Use leftover cinnamon mixture on cinnamon toast, or save in an airtight container for future muffins.

MICROWAVE LUNCHBOX HELPERS

Δ Soup, leftover stew or baked beans heat quickly in the morning in the microwave. Spoon into a thermos.

Δ For fast egg salad – crack egg into a small bowl. Pierce the yolk with a fork and cover the bowl with plastic wrap. Microwave on Medium for 1 1/2 to 2 minutes, or until yolk is almost set. Let stand 2 minutes to finish cooking. Mash and make your sandwich.

Δ For a marinated salad, combine leftover microwave-cooked vegetables with your favourite vinaigrette. Pack in small, leakproof containers.

Regular Oven Method – STRAWBERRY RHUBARB MUFFINS

Change baking powder amount to 2 1/2 teaspoons (12 mL). Eliminate cinnamon-sugar mixture. Bake at 375° F (190° C). for 20 to 25 minutes, or until muffins are golden brown.

MICROWAVE HINT FOR MUFFINS AND CAKES

Since baked goods do not brown in the microwave, sprinkle the tops of muffins or cakes with finely chopped nuts or your favourite streusel-type mixture.

MICROWAVE HINTS – MUFFIN BAKING

For even cooking, arrange small bowls used to bake muffins or cupcakes in a circle in the microwave. Rotate the bowls halfway through cooking if the muffins seem to be cooking unevenly. Remove muffins or cupcakes from baking pan(s) immediately after cooking and place on a rack to cool.

STRAWBERRY RHUBARB MUFFINS

A colourful breakfast treat using the first two fruits of summer.

1 3/4 cups	flour	425 mL
1 tablespoon	baking powder	15 mL
1/2 teaspoon	salt	2 mL
1/2 cup	sugar	125 mL
1/3 cup	oil	75 mL
1	egg	1
3/4 cup	milk	175 mL
3/4 cup	finely chopped fresh rhubarb	175 mL
1/2 cup	chopped, fresh strawberries	125 mL
1/4 teaspoon	cinnamon mixed with	1 mL
1 1/2 tablespoons	brown sugar	20 mL

1. Mix together flour, baking powder, salt and sugar in a large bowl.

2. Mix oil, egg and milk in a smaller bowl, then add liquid mixture to dry mixture. Stir just enough to moisten; do not overmix. Stir in the fruit.

3. Place muffin papers in a microwave muffin pan or in small microwave-safe bowls.

4. Fill each paper half-full with batter. Sprinkle a bit of the cinnamon mixture on each muffin. Microwave 6 muffins at a time on High for 1 3/4 to 2 1/2 minutes, or until muffins test done with a toothpick. Continue to cook 6 muffins at a time until the batter is used up.

Makes about 16 muffins.

PEACH AND CANTALOUPE CONSERVE

When winter winds blow, you'll be glad you took the time in the summer to make this sunny, sweet conserve. It will brighten your January breakfasts and brunches.

2 cups	peeled, diced cantaloupe	500 mL
2 cups	peeled, diced peaches	500 mL
1 1/2 cups	sugar	375 mL
2 teaspoons	orange zest	10 mL
3 tablespoons	orange juice	50 mL
1/4 cup	chopped candied cherries (optional)	50 mL

1. Combine cantaloupe, peaches, sugar, zest and juice in a 12-cup (3 L) microwave-safe casserole. Stir well. Cover and microwave on High for 8 minutes. Stir once during this time.

2. Microwave, uncovered, on High for 20 minutes, stirring occasionally, until the mixture thickens. Test thickness by placing a small amount of the conserve on a cold plate and placing it in the freezer for 2 minutes. If it has thickened slightly after this time, it is done. (A conserve is not as thick as jam). Stir in cherries if desired.

3. Spoon hot conserve into hot, sterilized small jars and seal with melted paraffin. Store in a cool, dark place.

Makes about 2 1/2 cups (625 mL).

SOMETHING YOUR MICROWAVE CAN'T DO

Because paraffin contains neither fat nor moisture (necessary to attract microwaves), it will not melt in the microwave. Melt the paraffin in a small jar or tin set in a larger pan of simmering water on the stovetop.

FREEZING RASPBERRIES

Arrange clean berries in a single layer on a jelly roll pan in the freezer. Once they are frozen, scoop them into bags, seal well and freeze. Removing only as much as you need is easy when the berries are frozen in this loose-pack way. Add a few frozen raspberries to fresh fruit salad, or to the filling when you are making apple or peach pies.

MICROWAVE HINT – AVOIDING JAM BOILOVERS

When you make jam in the microwave, always use a cooking container at least 3 times the volume of the quantity you are cooking. Jams and jellies boil up and over very quickly.

RASPBERRY JAM

Make several small batches of this jam to prevent boiling over in the microwave. The sugar can be decreased to 1 cup (250 mL) if you prefer less sweetness. This recipe also works well with strawberries, or both kinds of berries together.

4 cups	fresh raspberries	1 L
1 1/4 cups	sugar	300 mL
1 teaspoon	fresh lemon juice	5 mL

1. Place berries, sugar, and lemon juice in a 12-cup (3 L) casserole with a lid. Stir to mix. Cover with lid or vented plastic wrap and microwave on High for 8 minutes. Stir once during this part of the cooking time.

2. At the end of 8 minutes, stir well, then microwave on High, uncovered, for 10 to 15 minutes more, or until the mixture has thickened. Stir occasionally. Test thickness by placing a small amount of jam on a cold plate in the freezer for 2 minutes. It will thicken if it is ready.

3. Pour the mixture into hot, sterilized jars.

4. Melt paraffin on the stove in a heatproof bowl or clean, empty can set in a larger pan of simmering water. Paraffin will not melt in the microwave.

5. Top each jar with a thin layer of melted paraffin. Seal and store in a cool place.

Makes 2 to 2 1/2 cups (500 to 625 mL).

Three Fruit Marmalade

This recipe, adapted from *Master Your Microwave* by Glenda James, was first printed in response to a reader request. It is easy to make and is quite delicious.

1	grapefruit	1
1	orange	1
1	lemon	1
3/4 cup	water	175 mL
1/8 teaspoon	baking soda	0.5 mL
1/2	package (8 teaspoons [40 mL]) powdered pectin	.5
2 1/2 cups	sugar	625 mL

1. Peel and chop fruit and finely slice rind. Set fruit aside.

2. Place rind, water and baking soda in a 12-cup (3 L) casserole. Microwave on High for 8 minutes.

3. Add fruit and pectin crystals and microwave on High for 6 minutes.

4. Add sugar and microwave on Medium for 20 minutes, or until mixture thickens. Stir every 5 minutes. Test for doneness by putting a small amount of marmalade on a chilled plate and placing in the freezer for 2 minutes. Marmalade is ready when it is the desired thickness after this chilling time.

5. Cool slightly, then pour into sterilized jars. Seal with paraffin wax.

Makes 3 cups (750 mL).

Microwave Hint – Covering Leftovers

A heatproof glass casserole lid makes a perfect cover for reheating a dinner plate of leftovers in the microwave.

The Best of
SANDWICHES, SOUPS & SAUCES

CHUNKY PIZZA SOUP

This savoury meal-in-a-bowl is from *The Canadian Living Microwave Cookbook.* It's perfect for blustery fall or winter days.

1/2 cup	sliced mushrooms	125 mL
1/4 cup	slivered sweet green pepper	50 mL
1	small onion, chopped	1
1	clove garlic, minced	1
1 tablespoon	vegetable oil	15 mL
1	tin (28 ounces [796 mL]) tomatoes, undrained	1
1 cup	thinly sliced pepperoni, about 5 ounces (150 g)	250 mL
1/2 cup	beef stock	125 mL
1/2 teaspoon	dried basil	2 mL
	Salt and pepper	
1 cup	shredded mozzarella cheese	250 mL

1. In a 12-cup (3 L) casserole, combine mushrooms, green pepper, onion, garlic and oil. Cover and microwave at High for 3 to 5 minutes, or until softened, stirring once.

2. Stir in tomatoes, pepperoni, beef stock and basil. Cover and microwave at High for 10 to 15 minutes, or until flavours are blended and soup is heated through, stirring once. Season with salt and pepper to taste.

3. Ladle soup into 4 microwaveable soup bowls; sprinkle each with 1/4 cup (50 mL) of the cheese. Microwave, uncovered, at Medium for 1 to 1 1/2 minutes or until cheese melts. Serve immediately.

Makes 4 servings.

MICROWAVE HINT

Heating single servings of soup right in the bowl makes time-saving sense. Make sure that the soup bowl you use is microwave-safe (heatproof, no metal trim).

"CLEAN THE REFRIGERATOR" SOUP

We have a variation of this soup for dinner at least once a week in the winter. It provides a chance to use up leftovers and, served with crusty rolls or homemade bread and cheese, makes a delicious meal.

4 cups	chicken stock	1 L
1	onion, minced	1
3 to 4 cups	canned Italian plum tomatoes	750 mL to 1 L
1	stalk celery, sliced	1
1	large carrot, peeled and sliced thinly	1
1/2 cup	barley	125 mL

Leftovers such as:

	a few slices roast pork, beef, chicken or meatloaf, diced	
1/2 cup	leftover gravy	125 mL
1	small wedge cabbage, diced	1
2	cooked potatoes, diced	2
	Handful cooked, chopped pasta (sauce too, if you like)	
	Bit of parsley	
	Frozen vegetables such as peas, corn, beans	

1. Combine all ingredients except green vegetables in a large microwave-safe casserole and stir to mix well. Cover and microwave on High for 15 minutes, or until boiling. Stir, cover and microwave on Medium-low for 30 minutes, or until vegetables and barley are almost tender. Stir occasionally.

2. Stir in green vegetables, cover and microwave on High for 15 minutes, or until vegetables and barley are tender. Season with salt and pepper to taste. Sprinkle each serving with freshly grated Parmesan cheese. Serve with homemade bread and a variety of cheeses for a satisfying meal.

Makes 8 to 10 servings.

MICROWAVE HINT

Heat soup in microwave-safe serving bowls for a nutritious and quick after-school snack in cold weather. The bowl gets hot as the soup heats, so use oven mitts to take it out of the microwave.

CRABMEAT CHOWDER

Serve this after your next skating or toboganning party, with crusty rolls or cheese breadsticks and raw vegetables with a tangy dip.

2 cups	chicken stock	500 mL
1	tin crabmeat, reserve liquid	1
2 cups	milk	500 mL
1 tablespoon	butter	15 mL
3	strips bacon, diced	3
1/4 cup	minced onion	50 mL
2 tablespoons	flour	25 mL
1	large potato, peeled and finely diced	1
2 tablespoons	brandy or dry sherry (optional)	25 mL
	Salt and pepper to taste	
	Worcestershire sauce to taste	
1/2 cup	light cream	125 mL
	Chopped parsley to garnish	

1. Combine stock, crabmeat liquid and milk in a large microwave-safe casserole. Microwave on High for 5 minutes, or until just boiling. Stir once during heating. Set aside.

2. Place butter, bacon and onion in a 4-cup (1 L) glass measure. Microwave on High for 4 to 5 minutes or until bacon is crisp and onion is light brown. Stir once during cooking. Drain off 1 tablespoon (15 mL) bacon fat if desired.

3. Stir flour into bacon mixture and microwave on High for one minute. Whisk 1 cup (250 mL) of the hot liquid into the bacon mixture then stir this mixture into the rest of the hot liquid. Add potatoes. Cover and microwave on Medium for 10 minutes, or until potatoes are almost tender. Stir after 5 minutes.

4. Add brandy or sherry if desired. Stir in crabmeat and cream and season to taste with salt, pepper and Worcestershire sauce. Microwave on Medium-low for 5 minutes, or until hot but not boiling. Garnish each serving with minced fresh parsley.

Makes 5 to 6 servings.

MICROWAVE HINT

Using your microwave to make cream sauce and soup base will eliminate the difficult clean-up which results when milk burns on the bottom of the saucepan.

CREAM OF PECAN SOUP

An elegant way to start a meal. Your guests will probably not be able to guess what's flavouring the soup.

2 tablespoons	butter	25 mL
1/2 cup	finely chopped onion	125 mL
3 tablespoons	flour	25 mL
2 cups	chicken stock	500 mL
1 cup	ground pecans	250 mL
1 1/2 cups	milk	375 mL
	Freshly grated nutmeg to taste	
	Salt and pepper to taste	

1. Melt butter in an 8-cup (2 L) glass measure on High for 45 seconds. Stir in onion and microwave on High for 3 minutes, or until onion is soft.

2. Add flour, then gradually whisk in stock. Microwave on High for 5 minutes, stirring twice, until mixture is boiling and thickened.

3. Add pecans and milk and microwave on High for 3 minutes, or until heated through. Stir occasionally. Season to taste with nutmeg, salt and pepper. Serve hot.

Makes 4 to 6 servings.

MICROWAVE HINT – TOASTING NUTS IN THE MICROWAVE

You can toast nuts quickly in the microwave, with or without added butter or other fat. Place 1/2 cup (125 mL) of nuts in a microwave-safe dish and microwave on High. Check and stir every minute, until nuts are toasted to your liking. Record how long it took in your microwave cookbook for quick reference next time. Toss a few toasted walnuts or hazelnuts into a green salad, then add a few drops of walnut or hazelnut oil to the vinaigrette for a fabulous flavour change.

FRENCH ONION SOUP

Serve this soup as a light meal with a salad and crusty rolls, heated in the microwave. (6 rolls, High power for about 30 seconds.)

2 cups	sliced Spanish onion	500 mL
2 tablespoons	butter	25 mL
1	clove garlic, minced	1
3 cups	boiling beef stock	750 mL
	Salt and pepper to taste	
1/4 cup	brandy or cognac (optional)	50 mL
4 cups	grated mozzarella	1 L
6	rusks or slices of toasted French bread	6
	Grated Parmesan and paprika	

1. Combine onion, butter and garlic in a large microwave-safe casserole. Cover with plastic wrap and microwave on High for 6 to 8 minutes or until onion is soft. Stir once during cooking if desired.

2. Add beef stock and seasonings. Cover and microwave on High for 6 to 7 minutes, or until boiling hot. Stir in brandy.

3. Put 1/4 cup (50 mL) mozzarella in the bottom of each of 6 onion soup bowls. Pour in soup. Put rusk or bread slice in each bowl, then top with remaining mozzarella. Sprinkle with Parmesan and paprika. Microwave 3 bowls at a time on High for 3 to 5 minutes, or until cheese melts. Serve hot.

For a single serving, microwave on High for 1 to 1 1/2 minutes.

Makes 6 servings.

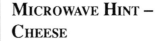

MICROWAVE HINT – CHEESE

Because prolonged microwave cooking makes cheese tough, do not put cheese on top of a dish before cooking. Whenever possible, layer the cheese into the dish, or place it on top near the end of the cooking time.

FRESH MUSHROOM CONSOMMÉ WITH ROSEMARY

The subtle flavor and sophisticated look of this soup make it an excellent first course for an elegant dinner.

4 cups	chicken stock	1 L
8 ounces	fresh mushrooms, finely minced	250 g
1/2 teaspoon	fresh rosemary leaves, or to taste	2 mL
	Salt and freshly ground pepper to taste	
	Thin mushroom slices to garnish	

1. Microwave stock, minced mushrooms and rosemary on High for 5 minutes or until boiling. Microwave, uncovered, on Medium for 15 minutes.

2. Strain consommé and discard the mushrooms and rosemary (or save and use in spaghetti sauce). Season to taste with salt and pepper. If the consommé appears cloudy, clarify it by straining it through a clean, fine cloth or a coffee filter.

3. Refrigerate until cold or serve hot, garnished with mushroom slices.

Makes 4 servings.

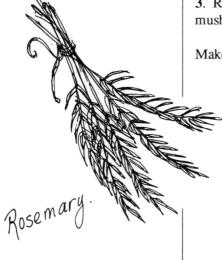

Rosemary.

Minestrone Soup

Freeze individual servings of this substantial soup for quick meals on busy evenings.

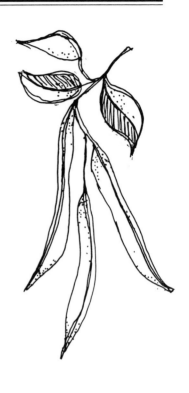

2 tablespoons	olive oil	25 mL
2	cloves garlic, minced	2
1 cup	chopped onion	250 mL
1 cup	thinly sliced celery	250 mL
1 cup	thinly sliced carrot	250 mL
1/2 to 1 cup	chopped zucchini	125 to 250 mL
1 cup	sliced green beans	250 mL
4 cups	chicken or beef stock	1 L
1	tin (19 ounce [540 mL]) undrained tomatoes, or 2 cups (500 mL) seeded chopped fresh tomatoes	1
2 tablespoons	fresh parsley, preferably Italian	25 mL
1/2 teaspoon	dried basil leaves	2 mL
1	tin (19 ounces [540 mL]) drained cooked white beans (or 2 cups freshly cooked)	1
1/3 cup	small shell pasta or broken spaghetti	75 mL
	Freshly ground pepper and salt to taste	
	Freshly grated Parmesan cheese	

1. Combine oil, garlic, onion, celery and carrot in a large microwave-safe casserole or simmer pot. Microwave on High for 3 to 5 minutes, or until vegetables are becoming tender.

2. Stir in zucchini, green beans, stock, tomatoes, parsley and basil. Cover and microwave on High for 10 to 12 minutes, or until mixture comes to a boil. Stir, then microwave on High for 10 to 15 minutes, stirring occasionally.

3. Stir in beans and pasta. Cover and microwave on Medium for 8 to 10 minutes, or until pasta is tender. Stir occasionally.

4. Season to taste, then serve at once or freeze for future use. Sprinkle each serving with freshly grated Parmesan cheese.

Makes 8 servings.

Wild Rice Soup

This is an excellent way to stretch 2/3 cup (150 mL) wild rice to serve 6.

5 cups	beef stock	1.25 L
1 tablespoon	cornstarch	15 mL
2 tablespoons	butter	25 mL
1 cup	thinly sliced mushrooms	250 mL
1/2 cup	finely chopped carrot	125 mL
1/2 cup	thinly sliced celery	125 mL
1/2 cup	minced onion	125 mL
2/3 cup	wild rice	150 mL
1/2 teaspoon	dried thyme leaves	2 mL
1	bay leaf	1
	Salt and pepper to taste	
	Parsley to garnish	

1. Mix the cornstarch with one cup of stock and set aside.

2. Place butter, mushrooms, carrot, celery and onion in a large casserole. Microwave on High for 5 to 6 minutes or until carrot is tender.

3. Add remaining 4 cups of stock along with rice, thyme, and bay leaf. Cover and microwave on High for 6 to 7 minutes or until mixture comes to a boil. Reduce power to Low and cook for 30 minutes, or until rice is tender and vegetables are cooked.

4. Stir in the cornstarch mixture. Microwave on High for 5 minutes or until soup thickens slightly. Stir twice during this cooking stage.

5. Remove bay leaf. Season to taste with salt and pepper and serve, garnished with minced fresh parsley.

Makes 6 servings.

AFTER SCHOOL PIZZA BUNS

This is one of my son Brian's favourite microwave "fast foods." It's perfect for after school or Saturday lunch, or anytime you want a nutritious nibble in a hurry. It is also a good first effort for new microwave owners.

1	hot dog, hamburger, or other bun, split in half	1
1 tablespoon	ketchup or tomato sauce	15 mL
	Oregano, garlic salt and pepper	
	Mozzarella cheese, shredded or thinly sliced	
	Toppings of your choice: pepperoni, ham, green pepper or mushrooms	

1. Place the two bun halves cut-side-up on a paper or microwave-safe plate.

2. Spread buns with tomato sauce or ketchup and sprinkle lightly with oregano, garlic salt and pepper. Add mozzarella to cover bun, and sprinkle with the toppings you have chosen.

3. Microwave on High for 1 minute, or until the cheese is melted and bubbly.

Makes 2 pieces.

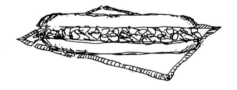

MICROWAVE HINT – FOOD ARRANGEMENT FOR EVEN COOKING

The arrangement of food is crucial to even cooking in the microwave. If a number of small items (such as potatoes, sandwiches or individual creme caramels) are to be cooked at the same time, arrange them in a circle in the microwave, leaving the center of the circle empty. Partway through cooking, rearrange the pieces so that the side facing the center is turned to face the walls of the oven. Similarly, if chicken or fish pieces are being cooked in a baking dish, arrange the pieces so that the thickest part of the piece faces the outer edge of the dish. Check partway through cooking, and rearrange pieces, placing the less cooked part to face the outer edge of the dish.

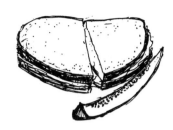

MICROWAVE HINT – MICROWAVE COOKWARE

For the benefit of children and part-time cooks in your family, identify containers that are microwave-safe by marking them with indelible markers.

MICROWAVE HINT – WRAPPING SANDWICHES

Wrapping sandwiches in a paper towel before heating in the microwave will give the bread a softer, more moist texture. Only a very brief heating time is needed – 10 to 20 seconds on High is usually enough.

HOT TUNA SUBS

Let your child make these for lunch or an after school snack. Kids like to use the microwave because it delivers fast results.

1	tin tuna, drained	1
1/2 cup	cubed cheddar cheese	125 mL
2 tablespoons	sweet pickle relish	25 mL
1/4 cup	finely chopped celery	50 mL
1/3 cup	mayonnaise, or enough to moisten	75 mL
	Salt and pepper to taste	
4	hot dog or hamburger rolls	4

1. In a small bowl, mix together the tuna, cheese, relish, celery and mayonnaise. Season to taste with salt and pepper. Spread one quarter of the mixture on each bun.

2. Wrap each bun in a paper towel. Microwave one at a time on High for 30 seconds, or until cheese melts.

Makes 4 servings.

REUBEN SANDWICH

A Reuben for Saturday lunch always brings a smile to my husband Read's face.

2	slices of your favorite rye or pumpernickel bread, buttered
	Mustard, regular, German or French
	Several slices smoked meat, corned beef or pastrami
	Swiss cheese slices
	Sauerkraut

1. Spread mustard on one of the bread slices and top with a generous layer of smoked meat. Cover the meat with sauerkraut. Place a layer of cheese on the other bread slice and leave the sandwich open on a serving plate.

2. Microwave on High for 1 minute or until the sandwich is heated through and the cheese is melted. Serve hot, garnished with a dill pickle.

Makes 1 serving.

HOT SUBMARINE SANDWICHES

In some areas, this sandwich is called a Hoagie. Let each person make their own with ingredients that suit their tastes.

1	hot dog or submarine sandwich roll, buttered
	Mustard, mayonnaise, ketchup, as desired
	Several types of cold meats: ham, beef, salami, sliced chicken, or your favourites
	Sliced cheese, your favourite
	Oregano, freshly ground pepper
	Slices of tomato and cucumber
	Shredded lettuce

1. Spread the opened roll with your choice of condiments. Top with the types and amounts of meat and cheese that you prefer. Sprinkle with oregano and pepper.

2. Place the still open sandwich on a serving plate and microwave on High for 45 seconds to 1 minute, or until the cheese melts.

3. Top with tomato, cucumber and lettuce. Close the sandwich and serve at once.

Variation: use whole wheat pita breads instead of the submarine rolls.

Makes 1 serving.

MICROWAVE HINT – PEANUT BUTTER

To soften peanut butter for easier spreading, remove the lid from the glass (not plastic) jar and microwave on High for 30 seconds to 1 minute, or until smooth.

MEXICAN BEAN BURRITOS

Flour tortillas can be found in the refrigerator or freezer sections of stores that sell a variety of Mexican foods and ingredients.

1	tin refried beans	1
2 tablespoons	finely minced onion	25 mL
	Chili powder and garlic salt, to taste	
2 tablespoons	taco sauce or water to moisten	25 mL
5 to 6	large flour tortillas	5 to 6
1 1/2 cups	shredded Monterey Jack or colby cheddar cheese	375 mL
	Toppings: taco sauce, shredded lettuce, chopped tomato, sour cream	

1. Mix beans and onion together in a 4-cup (lL) glass measure. Microwave on High for 2 minutes, or until heated through. Stir occasionally during cooking. Add chili powder and garlic salt to taste, and enough taco sauce or water to make mixture easy to spread.

2. Spread bean mixture evenly on the tortillas. Sprinkle with cheese and roll into a fairly tight roll, folding the ends under to prevent dripping.

3. Place on individual serving plates and microwave one at a time on High for 1 minute, or until heated through. Let each person garnish his own burrito.

Makes 5 to 6 burritos.

MICROWAVE LUNCHBOX HINT

When you have hot sandwiches for supper, make an extra to heat in the office microwave for lunch the next day. Carry raw vegetable garnishes separately to add to sandwich after heating.

Carol's Teriyaki Sauce

This sauce doubles as a marinade and is equally delicious on pork chops, ribs or kebobs, or on chicken pieces.

1/2 cup	sugar	125 mL
1 teaspoon	ground ginger	5 mL
1/4 teaspoon	salt	1 mL
1/4 cup	vinegar	50 mL
1/2 cup	soy sauce	125 mL
1 tablespoon	cornstarch	15 mL
1 tablespoon	water	15 mL
	Garlic to taste	

1. Mix all ingredients in a 4-cup (1 L) microwave-safe bowl or measuring cup. Microwave on High for 2 to 4 minutes, or until sauce is thick. Stir twice during cooking.

2. Cool sauce slightly before using as a marinade. Refrigerate the marinating meat for at least 2 hours before barbecuing.

3. Brush meat with reserved marinade during cooking. Use this procedure for meat which is not being precooked in the microwave. The sauce can also be used as a basting sauce for meat precooked in the microwave. Before using it as a basting sauce, microwave sauce on High for 3 minutes. This amount of sauce is enough for 8 pork chops or 6 to 8 serving pieces of chicken.

Makes about 1 cup (250 mL) of sauce.

Microwave BBQ Hint

Foods such as poultry benefit from precooking in the microwave, as the time required to complete the total cooking process on the barbecue can dry out the meat. Spareribs and other thick pork cuts, which must be well cooked for safety reasons, can also be partially cooked in the microwave to help to retain moisture. Follow the charts in the cookbook which came with your microwave to determine how long to precook. With poultry and ribs, add some water to the cooking container to ensure that the meat stays moist. I prefer to cook poultry and pork in the microwave until it is almost fully cooked, brush it with a flavourful basting sauce, then barbecue it just long enough to crisp and brown it.

CREAM SOUP OR SAUCE BASE

Use this versatile base to make cream of chicken or vegetable soup, cheese sauce for macaroni, seafood or herb sauce, or chicken à la king. Using a whisk to stir when adding milk ensures smoothness.

4 tablespoons	butter	50 mL
4 tablespoons	flour	50 mL
3 cups	milk	750 mL

1. Place butter in a large glass measuring cup or bowl. Microwave on High 40 seconds, or until melted. Stir in flour all at once. Slowly whisk in milk until well blended. Microwave on Medium for 8 to 10 minutes, stirring every 2 minutes, until sauce is hot and thickened.

2. Make sauce base as indicated, then add the appropriate amount of your favourite cooked, pureéd vegetables, cooked chopped chicken, shrimp, beef or pasta. Add herbs and spices that will best enhance the combination you have created. Add more milk to desired thickness.

Makes about 3 cups (750 mL) of soup base.

MICROWAVE HINT

Stirring with a whisk rather than a spoon will keep lumps from forming in sauces. Whisking will also help remove lumps. A plastic microwave-safe whisk is a handy tool, as it can be left in the dish during cooking when frequent stirring is needed.

FREEZER SPAGHETTI SAUCE

Make and freeze several batches of this sauce in the summer when tomatoes, onions and herbs are at their best. This is an all-purpose tomato sauce, excellent for use in casseroles, soups or sauces.

2 cups	chopped onion	500 mL
2	large cloves garlic, minced	2
1/3 cup	olive oil	75 mL
12 cups	chopped tomatoes (peeled before chopping; see note)	3 L
2 cups	dry red wine (or water)	500 mL
1 1/2 cups	tomato paste	375 mL
2	beef cubes, crumbled	2
4 teaspoons	dried basil, or 1/4 cup (50 mL) fresh, chopped basil leaves	20 mL
2	bay leaves	2
2 teaspoons	salt	10 mL

1. Place onion, garlic and oil in a large microwave simmer pot or casserole. Microwave on High for 5 minutes, or until onion is soft.

2. Add remaining ingredients. Cover and microwave on High for 12 minutes. Stir, cover, and microwave on Medium-low for 1 hour, stirring occasionally.

3. Remove bay leaves and cool slightly. Spoon mixture into serving-size containers, seal, label and freeze. To serve as a pasta sauce for 4 people, combine 2 to 4 cups (500 mL to 1 L) of sauce with 1 small tin of tomato paste and 12 ounces to 1 pound (350 to 500 g) of cooked meat, fish or poultry. Sauce can also be used plain.

Makes 16 cups (4 L) of sauce.

TIMESAVING TIP – PEELING TOMATOES

To peel tomatoes easily, cut off and discard the stem end. Freeze tomatoes. When ready to use, hold the frozen tomatoes under cool running water and the skins will slip right off.

LESLIE'S MOM'S BARBECUE SAUCE

Leslie Beal Bloom, a Pembroke native, now a food writer in the Washington D.C. area, shared this recipe with me. It makes a large amount and will keep indefinitely if stored in the refrigerator.

1/2 cup	packed brown sugar	125 mL
1/3 cup	cider vinegar	75 mL
1/2 cup	Worcestershire sauce	125 mL
1 cup	strong coffee	250 mL
1 1/2 cups	ketchup	375 mL
1/2 cup	vegetable oil	125 mL

1. Combine first 4 ingredients in an 8-cup (2 L) glass bowl or measure. Whisk in ketchup and oil. Microwave on High for 3 minutes, or until boiling.

2. Stir mixture, then microwave on High for 3 minutes, or until boiling. Stir again, then microwave on Medium – low for 10 minutes to blend flavours.

3. Cool, then store in the refrigerator. Warm the sauce in the microwave before using.

Makes 4 cups (1 L).

BEARNAISE SAUCE

Serve with grilled beef roasts or steaks, or with fish.

1/4 cup	red wine vinegar	50 mL
1/4 cup	dry vermouth	50 mL
1 tablespoon	minced onion	15 mL
1 1/2 teaspoons	fresh tarragon leaves	7 mL
	(1/2 teaspoon [2 mL] dried)	
1/4 teaspoon	salt	1 mL
	Dash of pepper	
3	egg yolks	3
1/2 cup	butter, melted	125 mL

1. Place vinegar, vermouth, onion, tarragon, salt and pepper in a 1-cup (250 mL) glass measure. Microwave on High for several minutes, checking every minute, until the liquid is reduced to 2 tablespoons (25 mL). Cool slightly.

2. Place yolks in blender or food processor and process to blend. Add vinegar mixture to yolks and process to mix. Melt butter in a glass measure on High for 1 minute, or until melted.

3. With machine running, pour butter into yolk mixture in a slow steady stream. The sauce will thicken at once and is ready to use as soon as all the butter is added.

To make the sauce by hand: Reduce liquid in the microwave to 3 tablespoons (45 mL). Strain. Whisk yolks in a small glass bowl. Whisk in the strained vinegar mixture. Slowly add the melted butter to the yolk mixture, whisking continuously as you pour. If sauce is too thin, microwave on Medium for 10 seconds, then whisk again.

MICROWAVE HINT – SAUCES

Cook microwave sauces in a large glass measuring cup and store in the same cup in the refrigerator. At serving time, place cup in the microwave and reheat. Whisking during reheating will keep sauce smooth.

PESTO SAUCE FOR ALL SEASONS

The flavour of this sauce closely approximates pesto made with a large quantity of fresh basil leaves. Use it when fresh basil is unavailable.

1 1/2 tablespoons	pine nuts or walnuts	25 mL
1 cup	spinach leaves, washed, stems removed	250 mL
1/4 cup snipped	fresh parsley	50 mL
1 teaspoon	dried basil leaves	5 mL
1/4 teaspoon	salt	1 mL
6 tablespoons	olive oil	75 mL
1 1/2 tablespoons	soft butter	25 mL
6 tablespoons	freshly grated Parmesan cheese	75 mL

1. Place nuts in a small microwave-safe bowl.
Microwave on High for 2 to 3 minutes or until browned.
Stir occasionally during cooking.

2. Place nuts, spinach, parsley, basil, salt, oil and butter in blender or food processor and process until smooth.
Scrape down sides during processing.

3. Transfer spinach mixture to a bowl and stir in cheese.
If the mixture is too thick, stir in a teaspoon of hot water.

4. Serve Pesto Sauce at room temperature over hot pasta.
Cover and refrigerate leftovers. Will keep 1 week.

Makes about 1 cup (250 mL).

STORAGE HINT FOR HERBS

To retain the most flavour, store herb leaves whole and crumble them when you are ready to use them. Store dried herbs in a dark place in an airtight container.

MEXICAN HOT SAUCE

This is a good all-purpose sauce to use with all of your favourite Mexican foods.

l	dried red chili pepper	1
l/2 teaspoon	dried oregano	2 mL
l teaspoon	whole cumin seed	5 mL
3	cloves garlic, minced	3
l	tin (7 1/2 ounce,[213 mL]) tomato sauce	1
3 tablespoons	water	50 mL
l tablespoon	red wine vinegar	15 mL

1. Crush chili pepper, oregano and cumin with a mortar and pestle or grind in a blender.

2. Add garlic, tomato sauce, water and vinegar. Pour into a storage jar with a tight fitting lid and shake well to combine. Store in the refrigerator. Will keep for several weeks.

Makes 1 1/4 cups (300 mL).

Quick Tomato Sauce

This fresh tasting sauce can be served over hot cooked pasta plain or with added cooked beef, chicken or seafood.

l tablespoon	olive oil	15 mL
2	cloves garlic, minced	2
4	tomatoes, seeded and chopped	4
1	19-ounce (540 mL) tin Italian plum tomatoes and liquid, chopped (2 1/2 cups [625 mL])	1
l teaspoon	dried (l tablespoon [15 mL] fresh) chopped basil leaves	5 mL
1/8 teaspoon	cayenne, or to taste	0.5 mL
1/4 teaspoon	salt, or to taste	1 mL

1. Place olive oil and garlic in a large microwave-safe casserole or glass measuring cup. Microwave on High for 1 1/2 minutes, or until garlic begins to brown slightly. Stir in fresh tomatoes and microwave on high for 5 minutes, or until tomatoes are soft. Stir twice during cooking.

2. Stir in remaining ingredients except salt and microwave on High for 10 minutes, stirring occasionally during cooking. Add salt to taste.

Makes about 4 cups (1 L) sauce.

MINT SAUCE

Serve with grilled lamb, or stir into plain yogurt and use as a dipping sauce for lamb meatballs.

1/2 cup	white vinegar	125 mL
1/4 cup	sugar	50 mL
3/4 cup	chopped mint leaves	175 mL

1. Place ingredients in a 2-cup (500 mL) glass measure. Microwave on High for 2 minutes, or until mixture just begins to boil. Let stand for 1 hour before using.

Makes 1/2 cup (125 mL).

The Best of
VEGETABLE SIDE DISHES, SALADS, RELISHES, PICKLES & CONDIMENTS

ASPARAGUS WITH PINE NUTS

You can substitute toasted almonds for the pine nuts, if you wish.

1 pound	fresh asparagus	500 g
3 tablespoons	toasted pine nuts	50 mL
1/4 cup	olive oil	50 mL
1 tablespoon	lemon juice	15 mL
1	clove garlic, minced	1
1/4 teaspoon	dried oregano	1 mL
1/4 teaspoon	dried basil	1 mL
1/2 teaspoon	salt	2 mL
1/4 teaspoon	pepper	1 mL

1. Place asparagus in a microwave-safe loaf pan with half of the stems at each end of the pan. Sprinkle with water and cover pan with plastic wrap. Microwave on High for 5 to 7 minutes, or until crisp-tender.

2. To toast pine nuts, place them in a small microwave-safe glass dish and microwave on High for 3 to 5 minutes, or until toasted. Stir once during cooking.

3. Whisk remaining ingredients together and pour into a glass baking pan. Microwave on High for 1 minute, or until very hot. Add asparagus and toss gently to coat with the herb mixture. Microwave on High for 2 to 3 minutes, or until heated through.

4. Place asparagus on a serving platter and drizzle the herb mixture over. Top with toasted pine nuts and serve at once.

Makes 4 servings.

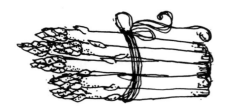

COOKING TIP – CHOOSING AND PREPARING ASPARAGUS

Choose asparagus with tightly closed heads and firm stalks with no signs of shrivelling: they are the freshest. Wash stalks. The light coloured bottom portion of the stem is often tough, so it should either be snapped off or peeled.

MICROWAVE HINT – STIRRING VEGETABLES DURING COOKING

Stir vegetables often during microwave cooking and they will cook more evenly.

MICROWAVE HINT – SAFETY WITH STEAMED FOODS

When you remove the lid or plastic wrap from dishes cooked in the microwave, you must be careful to avoid being burned by escaping steam. Cut a slit in the plastic wrap before removing it from the dish. When lifting off lids, be sure that your face is not in the way of escaping steam.

BROCCOLI MEDLEY

A colourful medley of flavours and textures. Serve it at your next dinner party and you'll get rave reviews.

4	slices bacon, cut into 1-inch (2.5 cm) pieces	4
1 tablespoon	butter	15 mL
1 cup	sliced mushrooms	250 mL
1	tin water chestnuts, drained and sliced	1
2 tablespoons	slivered almonds	25 mL
2 tablespoons	red pepper strips or chopped pimento	25 mL
1/2 teaspoon	salt	2 mL
1 pound	fresh broccoli spears, or 1 package (10-ounce (300 g) frozen	500 g
1/4 cup	chicken stock or water	50 mL

1. Microwave bacon on High in a microwave-safe pie plate for 3 to 4 minutes or until crisp. Stir twice. Set aside.

2. Place butter, mushrooms, water chestnuts, almonds, red pepper and salt in a large microwave-safe bowl or casserole. Microwave on High for 3 minutes, stirring once. Set aside.

3. Microwave broccoli and stock or water in a large covered casserole on High for 6 to 8 minutes or until crisp-tender. Stir occasionally. Recipe can be prepared to this point several hours ahead. Refrigerate each part separately.

4. Combine bacon with the two vegetable mixtures and microwave on High until hot (1 to 3 minutes if mixture is hot; 3 to 5 minutes if cold). Serve at once.

Makes 6 servings.

BROCCOLI AND CARROT CASSEROLE

*Quite popular
with Johnston's
& Holders
Mar 17, 2001*

Add this casserole to your Christmas dinner, or any other party menu. It's very colourful and tastes even better if assembled a day ahead.

4 cups	bitesize broccoli florets	1 L
4 cups	sliced carrots	1 L
	Water	
1/4 cup	butter	50 mL
1 cup	chopped onion	250 mL
1 teaspoon	salt, or to taste	5 mL
1/2 teaspoon	pepper	2 mL
1/4 cup	flour	50 mL
2 cups	sour cream	500 mL
1 tablespoon	melted butter	15 mL
1/3 cup	dry breadcrumbs	75 mL
1/3 cup	grated cheddar cheese	75 mL
	Paprika	

1. Cook broccoli with 1 tablespoon (15 mL) water in a tightly covered large glass measuring cup or casserole on High for 3 minutes, or until crisp-tender. Drain and transfer to a large bowl.

2. Place carrots and 1/4 cup (50 mL) water in the same cooking container, cover tightly and microwave on High for 6 minutes, or until carrots are crisp-tender. Drain and add to broccoli.

3. Place butter and onion in the same container and microwave on High for 3 minutes, or until onions are soft. Stir in salt, pepper and flour. Stir in sour cream and mix well. Microwave on High for 3 minutes, or until mixture is hot. Stir twice during heating.

4. Combine vegetables and sour cream mixture. Cover and refrigerate until serving time.

5. Combine melted butter and breadcrumbs. Cover and store in the refrigerator until needed.

6. At serving time, uncover the casserole and microwave on High for 7 to 9 minutes, or until heated through. Stir several times during heating.

7. Spoon vegetables into a heatproof serving dish and sprinkle crumb mixture over. Top with grated cheese and a sprinkling of paprika. Microwave on High just until cheese melts, or put under the broiler until cheese melts. Serve at once.

Makes 8 to 10 servings.

MICROWAVE HINT – PLASTIC WRAP

Even if plastic wrap is microwave-safe, it is better not to have it touching food while it cooks.

INDIVIDUAL CARROT FLANS

An elegant treatment for an everyday vegetable.

1 1/4 pounds	carrots, peeled and cut into 1-inch (2.5 cm) pieces	625 g
2 tablespoons	butter	25 mL
2	large eggs	2
1/2 cup	milk	125 mL
3 tablespoons	whipping cream	50 mL
1/2 teaspoon	freshly grated nutmeg	2 mL
1/4 teaspoon	salt	1 mL
	Pepper to taste	

1. Place carrots in a casserole with 1 cup (250 mL) water. Cover tightly and microwave on High for 9 to 14 minutes, or until carrots are soft. Stir once during cooking.

2. Drain carrots and purée in a food processor or blender with butter, eggs, milk, whipping cream and nutmeg. Taste and season with salt and pepper.

3. Pour purée into 6 buttered custard cups. Arrange filled cups in a circle in the microwave. Microwave on Medium-low for 7 1/2 to 9 minutes or until flans are set. Test by inserting a sharp knife into the center of one flan. It should come out clean. Let stand 5 minutes before unmoulding, or prepare ahead and reheat at serving time.

Makes 6 servings.

MICROWAVE HINT – DETERMINING COOKING TIME

If 2 cooking times are given for a dish, choose the shorter time, check the food when that time is up, then add more cooking time if needed. It is always better to undercook and add time, than to overcook and ruin the food.

CORN ON THE COB

Corn can be cooked in the microwave with or without husks. If you remove husks and silk, wrap corn in waxed paper or put in a covered casserole dish with a few drops of water. If you choose to leave husks on (the corn tastes sweeter if you do) take off the outer husks but be sure to leave at least two or three layers in place. Arrange cobs evenly in the microwave.

Microwave on High and rotate the cobs halfway through cooking.

Cook for the following times:

l cob - 2 to 3 minutes	2 cobs - 4 to 5 minutes
4 cobs - 7 to 9 minutes	6 cobs - 9 to 10 minutes

Let stand for 5 minutes before removing husks and silk.

GRILLED POTATO SLICES OR HALVES WITH MICROWAVE HELP

Try thyme, oregano or basil in place of the rosemary, and add garlic to the oil for an interesting change of taste.

l	large potato per person
	Vegetable or olive oil
	Salt and pepper to taste
	Fresh rosemary leaves if desired

1. Wash potatoes, prick them several times with a fork, and microwave on High until potatoes are almost tender to the center. (2 potatoes: cook for 5 minutes; 4 potatoes: 8 minutes; 6 potatoes: 10 minutes). Cut each potato into 3 or 4 large slices l/2-inch (1 cm) thick.

2. Pour a thin layer of oil onto a platter or jelly roll pan and sprinkle with salt, pepper and rosemary. Place potato slices on the oil mixture and turn over to coat both sides of the slices with oil mixture.

3. Arrange potato slices on the grill 4 to 6 inches (10 to 15 cm) above coals and cook 5 minutes on the first side. Turn over carefully and cook until second side is tender. If desired, brush potatoes with oil mixture as they cook.

MARINATED LEEKS

Serve this as the salad at your next dinner party. The leeks taste especially sweet when combined with a tangy mustard vinaigrette.

6	fresh leeks	6
1/4 cup	water	50 mL
3 tablespoons	tarragon vinegar	50 mL
1/2 teaspoon	paprika	2 mL
1/2 teaspoon	grainy French mustard	2 mL
1/8 teaspoon	cayenne (or to taste)	0.5 mL
1/2 teaspoon	salt	2 mL
1/2 cup	olive oil	125 mL

1. Trim off the root end and the tough green tops of each leek. Cut leeks in half lengthwise and wash carefully under cold, running water to remove all dirt.

2. Cut leeks into bitesize pieces and place in a microwave-safe casserole with water. Cover tightly and microwave on High for 6 to 8 minutes, or until leeks are crisp-tender. Stir several times during cooking. Drain leeks over a colander, shaking to remove all water. Pat dry.

3. Combine remaining ingredients in a jar with a tight fitting lid. Shake well to mix. Toss this mixture with leeks. Cover and refrigerate until cold. Can be prepared a day ahead.

Makes 4 to 6 servings.

MICROWAVE HINT – COVERING FOOD FOR COOKING

When a microwave recipe says to "cover tightly," the maximum amount of steam must be kept from escaping if the food is to cook evenly. Casserole lids do not usually seal well enough, so use microwave - safe plastic wrap for a really tight seal. This technique is the best one for cooking vegetables when little or no water is added.

RED CABBAGE AND APPLE

A German specialty that's delicious with roast pork or grilled pork chops.

6	slices of bacon, diced	6
1/2 cup	chopped onion	125 mL
5 cups	chopped red cabbage	1.25 L
1/4 to 1/2 cup	vinegar	50 to 125 mL
	Salt and pepper to taste	
1	large apple, peeled and chopped	

1. Put bacon and onion in a large microwave-safe casserole and microwave on High for 5 minutes, or until bacon is cooked and onion is soft. Add cabbage, cover and microwave on High for 5 to 6 minutes or until cabbage is crisp-tender. Stir once during cooking.

2. Add salt, pepper and 1/4 cup (50 mL) vinegar. Taste and add more vinegar if desired. Stir in apple. Microwave on High for 2 to 3 minutes, or until apples are tender but not mushy. Serve hot.

Makes 4 servings.

MICROWAVE HINT – REHEATING FOODS

By reheating a single serving rather than a whole dish of leftover food, you will avoid long cooking times which tend to overcook and dry out the food.

SAVORY GREEN BEANS WITH MUSHROOMS

This tasty vegetable side dish tastes delicious hot or cold.

1 pound	fresh or frozen green beans	500 g
4 ounces	fresh mushrooms, sliced	125 g
2 tablespoons	minced green onion	25 mL
2 tablespoons	butter	25 mL
1/4 cup	oil	50 mL
2 teaspoons	vinegar	10 mL
2 teaspoons	lemon juice	10 mL
2 teaspoons	minced parsley	10 mL
5 teaspoons	fresh or 1 1/2 teaspoons (7 mL) dried savory	25 mL
1/2 teaspoon	sugar	2 mL
1/2 teaspoon	salt	2 mL
1/8 teaspoon	pepper	0.5 mL
3	slices bacon, cooked, crumbled	3

1. Put beans in a large microwave-safe bowl or casserole. If beans are fresh, add 1/4 cup (50 mL) water. Cover with plastic wrap and microwave on High for 6 1/2 to 10 minutes (shorter time for fresh) or until beans are crisp-tender. Stir twice during cooking. Let stand 3 minutes, then drain and set aside.

2. Put mushrooms, onion and butter in a large microwave-safe bowl or casserole. Microwave on High for 2 to 3 minutes, or until onion is soft. Stir once. Add to beans; stir to mix. Set aside.

3. Place all remaining ingredients except bacon in a 1 or 2-cup (250 - 500 mL) glass measure. Microwave on High for 1 minute. Pour over hot bean mixture and toss gently. Spoon into a serving bowl and sprinkle with crumbled bacon. Serve at once. If you prepare this dish ahead, reheat on High for 3 to 4 minutes, or until heated through. Sprinkle with bacon just before serving.

Makes 4 to 6 servings.

SMOKED SALMON AND DILL STUFFED POTATOES

Usually regarded as a side dish, potatoes become the main attraction when prepared in this manner. Bake extras and freeze.

2	large baked potatoes, pulp scooped out, shells reserved	2
2 tablespoons	soft butter	25 mL
1/4 cup	cream cheese, softened	50 mL
2 tablespoons	sour cream	25 mL
1/2 cup	chopped smoked salmon	125 mL
2 tablespoons	fresh dillweed	25 mL
	Freshly ground black pepper to taste	
	Paprika to garnish	

1. Mash potato pulp with the butter, cream cheese, sour cream, smoked salmon and dillweed. Add pepper to taste.

2. Spoon filling into shells and sprinkle with paprika. Microwave on High for 2 minutes or until heated through.

Variation: substitute cooked shrimp or crabmeat for smoked salmon.

Leftovers can be frozen. Defrost and heat in the microwave.

Makes 2 servings.

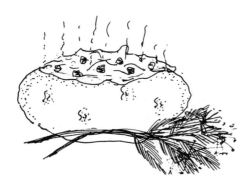

Regular Oven Method – SMOKED SALMON AND DILL STUFFED POTATOES

Bake at 425° F (220° C) for 30 minutes if cold, or 15 minutes if freshly made.

MICROWAVE HINT – BAKING POTATOES IN THE MICROWAVE

Wash potatoes, then prick each one several times with a fork or sharp knife. Arrange in a circle in the microwave and cook on High for the following times:

1 potato, medium size:
    3 1/2 to 4 minutes
2 potatoes:
    6 1/2 to 7 minutes
4 potatoes:
    10 to 11 minutes
6 potatoes:
    15 to 16 minutes

Rotate potatoes during cooking if your microwave doesn't have a turntable. Check often, and remove when a sharp knife inserts easily almost to the center. Let stand 5 minutes. Potatoes will finish cooking during standing time.

Regular Oven Method – SPINACH, BACON AND CHEESE STUFFED POTATOES

Bake stuffed potatoes at 425° F (220° C) for 30 minutes if cold, or 15 minutes if freshly made.

SPINACH, BACON AND CHEESE STUFFED POTATOES

Anyone with a microwave at their workplace can "brown-bag" one of these for a wonderful change from the everyday sandwich. Perfect for an after-school snack, a stuffed potato is quick, delicious and nutritious.

4	large baked potatoes, cut in half lengthwise, pulp scooped out, shells reserved	4
1 tablespoon	butter	15 mL
1/4 cup	chopped onion	50 mL
1/2 cup	cooked chopped spinach, squeezed dry (about 3 cups [750 mL] raw spinach)	125 mL
6	slices bacon, cooked and crumbled*	6
1	egg, slightly beaten	1
1 1/4 cups	grated cheddar cheese	300 mL
	Salt and pepper to taste	
	Paprika to garnish	

1. In a small bowl, microwave butter and onion on High for 2 minutes, or until onion is soft.

2. Add onion mixture to potato pulp along with spinach, bacon, egg, and 1 cup of the cheese. Mix well. Season to taste with salt and pepper.

3. Mound filling back into shells. Sprinkle with remaining cheese and paprika. Microwave on High for 3 minutes or until heated through.

*Substitute 1 1/2 cups (375 mL) thinly sliced ham for the bacon, if desired.

Note: Leftovers can be frozen. Defrost and heat in the microwave.

Makes 4 servings.

Vegetable Spaghetti Squash – How to Cook

Wash and dry squash and pierce skin several times with a sharp knife. Place on a microwave-safe plate on a paper towel (if the squash is coated with wax) and microwave on High for 5 to 7 minutes per pound (500 g), or until squash is tender when pierced with a fork or sharp knife. Turn squash over halfway through cooking. Let stand 5 minutes. Cut squash in half lengthwise and scoop out seeds. Use a fork to pull out and separate squash strands.

Use as a substitute for pasta, topped with your favorite Italian tomato sauce or Ratatouille, and freshly grated Parmesan cheese.

Turnip – How to Cook

Pierce skin of the turnip several times with a sharp knife. Weigh it and place it on paper towelling (to absorb wax as it melts off) on a microwave-safe plate. Microwave on High for 6 minutes per pound (500 g), or until tender when pierced with a sharp knife. Turn turnip over halfway through cooking time. Let stand for 10 minutes to finish cooking. Cool, then peel, chop and use in your favourite recipe.

Microwave Hint

Tasty topping for hamburgers and hot dogs: Slice a large Spanish onion and place in a casserole with 1 tablespoon (15 mL) butter or oil. Cover and microwave on High for 4 minutes, or until tender.

Regular Oven Method – ZUCCHINI STUFFED WITH BACON AND TOMATO

Bake at 375° F (190° C) for 30 minutes or until tender.

TOO MUCH ZUCCHINI ?

Grate and freeze extra in 1-cup (250 mL) quantities to defrost in the microwave and use in muffins, ground meat recipes, sauces or soups.

ZUCCHINI STUFFED WITH BACON AND TOMATO

This is an excellent side dish for grilled meat, fish or poultry. You can use small peeled cucumbers in place of the zucchini.

3	zucchini, 6 inches (15 cm) long	3
3	slices bacon	3
1/4 cup	chopped onion	50 mL
1/2 cup	chopped tomato	125 mL
1 or 2	shakes Tabasco sauce, or to taste	1 or 2
1/4 teaspoon	dried basil	1 mL
1/3 cup	dry breadcrumbs	75 mL
1/4 cup	freshly grated Parmesan cheese	50 mL
1/2 teaspoon	salt, or to taste	2 mL
	Freshly ground pepper	
2 teaspoons	butter	10 mL
	Paprika	

1. Wash zucchini and cut in half lengthwise. Scoop out seeds and discard them. Place zucchini halves, cut side up on a microwave-safe plate.

2. Chop bacon into 1/4-inch (6 mm) pieces. Place in a glass bowl along with onion and microwave on High for 6 minutes or until bacon and onion are crisp and brown. Drain off fat.

3. Mix tomato and Tabasco together, then add tomato mixture along with remaining ingredients except butter and zucchini shells to bacon mixture and stir well. Taste and adjust seasonings.

4. Spoon bacon mixture into zucchini shells. Dot with butter and sprinkle with paprika. Cover with microwave-safe plastic wrap or waxed paper and microwave on High for 8 to 10 minutes, or until zucchini is just tender but not soft. Rotate zucchini halves in the dish after 5 minutes if they seem to be cooking unevenly. Let stand 5 minutes before serving.

Makes 6 servings.

ARTICHOKE HEART SALAD

This delicious salad was on the menu when *Canadian Living* food editor, Elizabeth Baird, came to visit my cooking school.

1	recipe Italian Dressing (see below)	1
1/4 cup	chopped sweet red pepper or pimento	50 mL
1	tin artichoke hearts, drained	1
1	tin (2 ounces [62.5 g]) anchovy fillets, rinsed and chopped	1
6 cups	mixed salad greens	1.5 L

ITALIAN DRESSING:

1/2 cup	olive oil	125 mL
1/3 cup	vinegar	75 mL
2 tablespoons	water	25 mL
2	green onions, chopped	2
1 teaspoon	sugar	5 mL
1	clove garlic, crushed	1
1/4 teaspoon	celery seed	1 mL
	Salt and freshly ground pepper to taste	

1. Place dressing ingredients and red pepper in a large measuring cup or microwave-safe bowl. Microwave on High for 2 minutes, or until boiling.

2. Cut artichoke hearts into bitesize pieces. Stir them into the hot dressing and microwave on High for 1 to 2 minutes, or until artichokes are hot. Stir in anchovies. Refrigerate, covered, for at least 2 hours.

3. Wash and dry salad greens. Tear into bitesize pieces, wrap and refrigerate until serving time.

4. At serving time, drain and reserve vegetables and dressing. Toss vegetables with the greens, adding enough of the dressing to coat greens. Serve at once.

Makes 8 to 10 servings

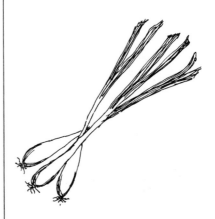

Egg Salad Mould

The flavour of this attractive side dish is similar to devilled eggs, but much faster to prepare. It makes a very attractive addition to a party buffet.

6	eggs	6
1/2 cup	mayonnaise	125 mL
1/2 cup	finely minced celery	125 mL
2 tablespoons	drained sweet pickle relish	25 mL
2 tablespoons	finely minced green onion	25 mL
1/4 cup	finely chopped sweet red pepper	50 mL
1 1/2 teaspoons	mustard	7 mL
	Salt and freshly ground pepper	
1 1/2 teaspoons	unflavoured gelatin (1/2 package)	7 mL
3 tablespoons	cold water	50 mL

1. Carefully break each egg into a small, lightly-oiled microwave-safe bowl. Do not break yolks, but pierce each yolk several times with a fork. Cover with plastic wrap and microwave each egg on Medium for 1 1/2 to 2 minutes, or until white is set and yolk is almost set. Let stand for 3 minutes before chopping. Repeat procedure with remaining eggs.

2. Cool eggs, then mash by hand or in food processor using an off - on pulse.

3. Combine chopped eggs with mayonnaise, celery, relish, onion, red pepper, mustard, salt and pepper. Add more mayonnaise if mixture is too dry.

4. Combine gelatin and water in a 1-cup (250 mL) measure. Microwave on Low for 1 minute, or until gelatin dissolves. Stir into egg mixture.

5. Pour egg mixture into a lightly-oiled 4-cup (1 L) mould. Cover and refrigerate 4 hours or overnight.

6. To unmould, run a sharp knife around top edge of mould to loosen. Immerse mould to 1 inch (2.5 cm) from top in a sink or bowl of hot water for 30 seconds to 1 minute. Dry mould and invert onto a serving platter. Remove mould and garnish salad with parsley and cherry tomatoes.

Makes 6 servings.

Microwave Hint – Exploding Eggs

Sometimes, even after you pierce the egg yolk before cooking in the microwave, it will still pop or explode during cooking. Overcooking causes this to happen, so try to undercook eggs slightly and let them finish cooking during the standing time.

FRENCH POTATO SALAD

Several readers have written to me requesting recipes for summer salads. Make this potato salad part of your next picnic menu – it contains no mayonnaise or egg, so is safer to carry in warm weather.

8	medium potatoes	8
2 tablespoons	minced fresh chives	25 mL
1/4 cup	white vinegar	50 mL
4 teaspoons	Dijon mustard	20 mL
3/4 cup	vegetable oil	175 mL
	Salt and pepper	

1. Scrub potatoes and prick each one several times with a fork or sharp knife. Arrange in a circle in the microwave. Microwave on High for about 20 minutes, or until potatoes are tender when pierced with a sharp knife. Peel potatoes when cool enough to handle, then chop into a large bowl. Stir in chives.

2. Place vinegar, mustard and oil in a jar with a tight-fitting lid and shake well. Add salt and pepper to taste.

3. Gently mix enough vinaigrette into potatoes to moisten. Season to taste. The salad can be covered and refrigerated if made ahead, but it is best served at room temperature, garnished with paprika.

Variation: Add 2 chopped hard-cooked eggs to the potato mixture before adding vinaigrette.

Makes 8 servings.

QUICK TIPS FOR THE MICROWAVE

Avocado – if hard and underripe, soften in the microwave on High for 1 minute, then cool completely before slicing or mashing.

Lemon – you can squeeze more juice from a lemon or any other citrus fruit if you microwave it on Medium for 30 seconds to 1 minute before squeezing.

Parsley

Try baking red potatoes for 8 min let set 2 min

MICROWAVE HINT – FOODS THAT EXPLODE IN THE MICROWAVE

Foods that are completely enclosed in a membrane will explode in the microwave if you fail to puncture the membrane several times with a fork or sharp knife. Some of these foods are potatoes, chicken liver, egg yolk, whole squash and oysters.

GERMAN POTATO SALAD *Nel not fond of it Not bad cold!*

When cooked, cubed potatoes are tossed with fried onions, bacon and a vinegar -based sauce, the resulting German potato salad makes a tasty addition to an Oktoberfest menu.

4	medium potatoes	4
5	slices bacon, chopped	
1	medium onion, chopped	1
2 tablespoons	flour	25 mL
2 tablespoons	sugar	25 mL
1/2 teaspoon	salt	2 mL
1/4 teaspoon	celery seed	1 mL
1/4 teaspoon	pepper	1 mL
1/3 cup	water	75 mL
1/2 cup	vinegar	125 mL
	Paprika	
	Minced fresh parsley	

1. Wash potatoes, prick several times with a fork and microwave on High for 8 to 10 minutes, or until tender. Cool, peel and dice.

2. Microwave bacon and onion in a large glass measuring cup on High for 8 to 10 minutes or until bacon is cooked and brown. Stir twice during cooking.

3. Combine sugar, flour and seasonings and stir into bacon mixture. Gradually stir in water and vinegar. Microwave on High for 2 minutes or until thick and bubbly. Stir occasionally.

4. Stir potatoes into bacon mixture and taste and adjust seasonings.

5. Spoon into a microwave-safe casserole. Sprinkle with paprika, cover and microwave on High for 4 minutes, or until heated through. Sprinkle with parsley and serve hot.

Makes 4 to 6 servings.

GREEN SALAD WITH WARM CHÈVRE

The hazelnuts for this recipe can be roasted in the microwave. Place in a small microwave-safe dish and microwave on High for 3 to 4 minutes or until toasted. Place between 2 layers of tea towel and rub to remove some of the skins from the nuts. Grind or chop as finely as possible by hand.

4 ounces	soft (fresh) goat cheese (chèvre)	125 g
1 tablespoon	olive oil	15 mL
1/4 cup	ground toasted hazelnuts or walnuts	50 mL
1	Boston lettuce, torn into bitesize pieces	
1	head radicchio, torn into bitesize pieces (optional)	
	Edible blossoms to garnish: violets, rose petals, nasturtiums, clover, or the blossoms of herbs such as chives, oregano, basil or thyme	

VINAIGRETTE:

1 1/2 tablespoons	tarragon vinegar	25 mL
1/2 teaspoon	Dijon mustard, or to taste	2 mL
1/3 cup	olive oil	75 mL
1 tablespoon	hazelnut or walnut oil	15 mL
	Salt and pepper to taste	

1. Cut cheese into 4 equal pieces. Coat each piece with oil, then coat with ground nuts. Arrange in a circle around the edge of a microwave-safe plate. Set aside.

2. Wash lettuce and radicchio and place in a large bowl. Wash blossoms and pat dry. Place in a small bowl.

3. Combine vinaigrette ingredients in a jar with a tight-fitting lid and shake well. Taste and adjust seasonings.

4. At serving time, microwave the cheese on Medium for 30 seconds to 1 minute, or until cheese just begins to melt.

5. Toss the greens with enough vinaigrette to coat. Spoon onto 4 individual salad plates. Sprinkle each serving with blossoms, and top with a slice of warm cheese. Serve at once.

Makes 4 servings.

Basil

JULIENNE CARROT SALAD WITH FRESH DILL

You will intensify the flavour of this salad if you make it early in the day and allow several hours for the individual tastes to come together.

l pound	carrots, peeled, cut in thin	500 g
	julienne strips (3 1/2 cups [875 mL])	
1 1/2 tablespoons	white wine vinegar	25 mL
1/4 cup	vegetable oil	50 mL
l tablespoon	chopped fresh parsley	15 mL
l tablespoon	minced fresh dillweed	15 mL
l tablespoon	minced green onions or chives	15 mL
l	small clove garlic, minced	1
1/4 teaspoon	salt	1 mL
	Freshly ground pepper	

1. Place carrot strips in a large microwave-safe casserole with 1/4 cup (50 mL) water. Microwave on High for 4 minutes, stirring once after 2 minutes. Place cooked carrots in ice water as soon as cooking is done, to refresh them and keep them from overcooking.

2. Combine vinegar, oil, parsley, dillweed, onions, garlic, salt and pepper in a jar with a tight-fitting lid and shake well to blend. Taste and adjust seasonings.

3. Pour dressing over carrots and mix well. Refrigerate at least 4 hours before serving. Can be made a day ahead.

Makes 4 to 6 servings.

MICROWAVE HINT – BLANCHING VEGETABLES

Though some vegetables can be used raw in marinated salads, others such as green beans, broccoli, and, in some cases, carrots, benefit from a quick blanching to improve their flavour, colour and texture. Blanching time in the microwave for one pound (500 g) of vegetables is usually one-half the time required to fully cook the vegetable.

HOT AND SWEET MUSTARD

Delicious with tourtière or ham, or on sandwiches or
sausage rolls. I have occasionally spooned this tasty
mustard into a decorative jar and taken it as a hostess gift
at Christmas time.

l/2 cup	dry mustard	125 mL
l/2 cup	sugar	125 mL
l/2 teaspoon	salt	2 mL
2 tablespoons	honey	25 mL
l tablespoon	vinegar	l5 mL
2 tablespoons	water	25 mL
2 tablespoons	orange marmalade	25 mL

1. Mix mustard, sugar and salt in a small bowl.

2. Mix honey, vinegar and water in a 1-cup (250 mL)
glass measure. Microwave on High for l minute, or until
boiling.

3. Stir honey mixture and mustard mixture together until
sugar dissolves. Stir in marmalade.

4. Spoon into a l-cup (250 mL) jar and refrigerate.

Makes 1 cup (250 mL).

MICROWAVE HINT – VEGETABLES AND SALT

Adding salt to the water when
you cook vegetables in the
microwave will cause them to
become shrivelled and tough.
Add salt after cooking.

MARTHA'S DILLS

One of the frustrations of growing your own pickling cucumbers is the length of time it takes to get enough ripe cucumbers to make a large batch of pickles. Solve this problem by making smaller batches in the microwave. This recipe can be prepared with a minimum of fuss. The original version was given to me by my friend Martha Stauch who lives in Kitchener, Ontario.

8 cups	small pickling cucumbers, scrubbed	2 L
4	cloves garlic	4
4	large fresh dill heads or blossoms	4
4 cups	water	1 L
1 cup	vinegar	250 mL
1/4 cup	coarse pickling salt	50 mL

1. Sterilize 2 1-quart (1 L) size sealers in boiling water. Into each hot sealer place half of the cucumbers, 2 cloves garlic, and 2 dill blossoms or heads.

2. Combine water, vinegar and salt in an 8-cup (2 L) measuring cup. Microwave on High for 8 to 10 minutes, or until brine is boiling. Pour boiling brine into the sealers over the cucumbers to 1/2-inch (1 cm) from top of jar. Seal with new canning jar lids and rings. Store in a cool, dry place for 6 weeks before using.

Makes 2 quarts (2 L).

MICROWAVE HINT – BLANCHING VEGETABLES

Many microwave cookbooks have time charts for blanching vegetables. The technique is simple.

1. Wash the vegetables and peel, slice, or chop them as you normally would for freezing. Place in cooking container with 1/4 cup (50 mL) water. Blanch in quantity indicated on the chart. If you do not have a blanching chart, blanch for 1/2 the time usually needed to cook that vegetable. Container should be tightly covered. Do not try to blanch too large a quantity at once, or vegetables will cook unevenly. Use High power and stir at least once during cooking.

2. At end of blanching time, place hot vegetables immediately in a sink full of ice cold water to stop the cooking process and keep the vegetables crisp. When vegetables become cold, drain and dry them well. Pack in desired quantity, label and freeze.

MIXED FRUIT CHUTNEY

This chutney is quite inexpensive and easy to make. It is delicious in sandwiches, especially sliced chicken, or as an accompaniment to poultry or ham. I like to heat it with half as much melted butter to use as a dipping sauce for chicken fingers.

1	orange, peeled, seeded, chopped	
1	lemon, peeled, seeded, chopped	1
2 cups	cider vinegar	500 mL
2 1/2 cups	firmly packed dark brown sugar	625 mL
1	clove garlic, minced	1
	Dash of ground cloves and cayenne	
1 teaspoon	chili powder	5 mL
1 1/2 teaspoons	salt	7 mL
1/2 cup	chopped crystallized ginger	125 mL
1 cup	chopped onion	250 mL
1 cup	currants	250 mL
1 cup	raisins	250 mL
2	apples, peeled, cored, chopped	2
3	peaches, peeled, chopped	3
2	pears, peeled, cored, chopped	2

1. Place all ingredients except apples, peaches and pears in a 12-cup (3 L) microwave-safe casserole. Microwave on High for 7 to 9 minutes, or until boiling. Stir once. Microwave on Medium for 20 minutes, stirring occasionally.

2. Add remaining fruit and microwave on Medium for 30 minutes, or until thick and syrupy.

3. Spoon into 6 hot, sterilized jars. Wipe the rims and seal with new canning lids and rings.

4. Process in a water bath for 10 minutes. Store in a cool, dark place for 4 weeks before using. Refrigerate jars after they are opened.

Makes 6 cups (1.5 L).

FOOD SAFETY TIPS

Consult a preserving cookbook about correct canning procedures for water bath processing.

Important note: You CANNOT process home canned goods in the microwave.

RASPBERRY VINEGAR

Use this tangy condiment in salads or sauces. Deglaze the pan with Raspberry Vinegar the next time you sauté pork or veal chops, or boneless chicken breasts.

2 cups	white wine vinegar	500 mL
1 cup	fresh raspberries	250 mL

1. Combine vinegar and berries in a 4-cup (1 L) glass measure or bowl. Microwave on High for 4 to 6 minutes, or until mixture comes to a boil. Remove from heat and cool. Cover with plastic wrap and refrigerate overnight.

2. The next day, strain vinegar through a fine sieve lined with several layers of damp cheesecloth. Avoid pressing the fruit through the sieve, or the vinegar will be cloudy.

3. Pour vinegar into small, hot, sterilized jars or bottles. Seal and store in a dark, cool place.

Makes about 2 cups (500 mL).

FRESH TOMATO SALSA

Be sure to wash your hands carefully after chopping the jalapeno pepper. The volatile oils in this type of pepper can cause a painful reaction to eyes and sensitive skin.

2	ripe tomatoes, seeded and diced	2
1/3 cup	chopped green pepper	75 mL
1/2 teaspoon	minced fresh garlic	2 mL
1	green onion, minced	1
1/4 cup	tomato juice	50 mL
1 1/2 teaspoons	chopped jalapeno peppers, or to taste	7 mL
1/2 teaspoon	dried oregano leaves	2 mL
2 teaspoons	fresh chopped cilantro (optional) or parsley	10 mL
	Salt to taste	

1. Combine all ingredients except salt and mix well. Add more tomato juice if you like juicier salsa. Taste and add salt as needed. Can be made a day ahead. Refrigerate until needed.

Makes about 1 cup (250 mL) salsa.

MICROWAVE HINT – REDUCING LIQUIDS

When a recipe tells you to "reduce" the liquid, do it in the microwave in a glass measuring cup. You will easily be able to see when you have the quantity that you need. Because the mixture will boil rapidly as it reduces, use a measuring cup that holds at least 4 times the quantity of liquid you start with.

TARRAGON VINEGAR

An excellent addition to your favourite vinaigrette. Can also be used as a marinade for chicken, or to deglaze the pan when cooking chicken.

l cup	loosely packed, fresh chopped tarragon leaves	250 mL
l 3/4 cups	white vinegar	425 mL
l/4 cup	dry white wine (or use 1/4 cup [50 mL] more vinegar)	50 mL

Note: you can substitute 2 cups (500 mL) white wine vinegar for the white vinegar and wine.

l. Put tarragon leaves in a clean jar.

2. Heat vinegar and wine in the microwave in a large measuring cup on High for 3 minutes, or until just below the boiling point.

3. Pour hot vinegar mixture over tarragon leaves. Put jar in a dark place (a kitchen cupboard is good) for 2 weeks, shaking the jar gently each day.

4. Strain vinegar through several layers of damp cheesecloth or a coffee filter and pour into small, sterilized jars. Add a sprig of fresh tarragon to each jar and seal. Store in a cool, dark place.

Makes 2 cups (500 mL).

SPIRITED CRANBERRY SAUCE

Another holiday treat, cooked and refrigerated in the same container to save time and dishes.

l/3 cup	orange juice	75 mL
l to l l/2 cups	sugar, or to taste	250 to 375 mL
1	package (12 ounces [350 g]) fresh or frozen cranberries	1
2 tablespoons	orange liqueur	25 mL
	Grated zest of l orange	

1. Place orange juice and sugar in a large microwave-safe casserole or measuring cup. Microwave on High for 2 minutes, or until sugar dissolves. Stir once during cooking.

2. Stir in cranberries. Microwave on High for 5 to 6 minutes, or until berries are soft, stirring once during cooking. Mash berries slightly.

3. Stir in liqueur and zest. Taste and add more sugar if needed.

4. Chill before serving. Can be made several days ahead and stored in the refrigerator.

Makes about 2 cups (500 mL).

GUACAMOLE

1	clove garlic, minced	1
2	ripe avocadoes	2
2 tablespoons	lime juice	25 mL
1/3 cup	finely chopped onion	75 mL
1/2 teaspoon	salt, or to taste	2 mL
1/2	of a small tin diced chillies	1/2
1/3 cup	finely diced tomato	75 mL

1. Purée garlic, avocado and lime juice in food processor or mash by hand. Stir in remaining ingredients. Taste and adjust seasonings. Cover and chill until needed.

Makes about 1 1/2 cups (375 mL).

The Best of
PASTA, GRAINS
& RICE

PASTA WITH CREAMY SMOKED SALMON SAUCE

A delectable sauce that can be put together in the time it takes to cook the pasta. Just the thing at the end of a busy day. You can substitute 12 ounces (350 g) dried pasta for the fresh.

3 tablespoons	butter	50 mL
4	green onions, chopped	4
1	small clove garlic, minced	1
8 ounces	smoked salmon, diced	250 g
3/4 cup	whipping cream	175 mL
3/4 cup	freshly grated parmesan cheese	175 mL
	Freshly ground pepper to taste	
1 pound	fresh fettucine, cooked and drained	500 g

1. Place butter, onions and garlic in a large microwave-safe bowl and microwave on High for 2 minutes, or until onions are soft.

2. Add salmon and microwave on High for 1 minute. Stir.

3. Add whipping cream and microwave on Low for 2 to 3 minutes, or until hot but not boiling.

4. Add hot pasta, cheese and some pepper to the sauce and toss to mix well. Spoon into a warm serving dish and serve at once with more cheese and pepper if desired.

Makes 4 servings.

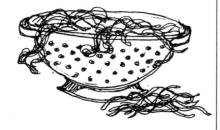

PASTA WITH FOUR CHEESES

This is one of my favourite pasta dishes. Change the cheeses to suit your own taste.

3 tablespoons	butter	50 mL
1/4 cup	flour	50 mL
1/2 teaspoon	salt	2 mL
	Dash of pepper	
2 1/2 cups	milk	625 mL
2/3 cup	grated mozzarella cheese	150 mL
2/3 cup	grated Swiss or Monterey Jack cheese	150 mL
2/3 cup	grated provolone cheese	150 mL
2/3 cup	grated Parmesan cheese	150 mL
12 ounces	fettucine, cooked and drained	350 g
2 tablespoons	grated Parmesan (second amount) Paprika	25 mL

1. Melt butter in an 8-cup (2 L) glass measure or casserole. Whisk in flour, salt and pepper.

2. Whisk in milk in a slow steady stream. Microwave on Medium for 7 to 10 minutes, whisking every 2 minutes, until sauce is hot and thickened.

3. Add all cheeses, except second amount of Parmesan, and continue to stir or whisk until cheeses melt. Microwave on Medium for 1 minute to finish melting if necessary.

4. Add hot, cooked pasta and stir to mix well. Taste and adjust seasonings.

5. Pour pasta mixture into a buttered 8-cup (2 L) casserole. Sprinkle Parmesan and paprika on top. Microwave on High for 3 to 5 minutes to heat through. Place under a broiler for 3 to 5 minutes or until top is brown and bubbly. Serve hot.

Makes 6 servings.

BUYING A NEW MICROWAVE ?

Take your largest microwave pot shopping with you to be sure that it will fit into the new microwave.

Sausage and Pepper Sauce for Pasta

For a more mellow flavour, prepare this dish a day ahead and reheat.

l pound	hot or sweet Italian sausages	500 g
l tablespoon	olive oil	15 mL
l	clove garlic, minced	1
l	medium onion, chopped	1
l	large green pepper, chopped	1
l	large red pepper, chopped	1
l	28-ounce (796 mL) tin Italian plum tomatoes, drained and coarsely chopped	1
l teaspoon	dried oregano	5 mL
	Few sprigs fresh parsley	
	Salt and pepper to taste	
	Freshly grated Parmesan	
	Hot cooked fettucine (1 pound [500 g] uncooked)	

1. Pierce each sausage several times with a sharp knife and arrange in a single layer in a glass baking dish. Cover loosely with waxed paper (to prevent splattering) and microwave on High for 7 minutes or until cooked through. Rearrange sausages partway through cooking. Drain well, discard pan drippings, then cut sausages into bitesize pieces.

2. Place oil, garlic and onion in an 8-cup (2 L) glass measure. Microwave on High for 4 minutes, or until onion is soft. Add green and red peppers and microwave on High for 3 minutes.

3. Stir in tomatoes, oregano, parsley and sausage pieces. Microwave on High for 7 minutes, or until sauce is boiling. Taste and add salt and pepper if needed.

4. Serve sauce on hot fettucine, sprinkled with freshly grated Parmesan cheese.

Makes 6 servings.

Microwave Hint

All foods which have a non-porous skin or which are enclosed in a membrane, must be pierced before cooking in the microwave to prevent bursting. Foods in this category include vegetables such as eggplant or squash, fruits such as apples, meats such as sausages, hot dogs and chicken livers, and egg yolks. Overcooking these foods will also cause some of them to explode, even if they have been pricked before cooking.

SUN-DRIED TOMATO CREAM SAUCE FOR PASTA

Assemble and cook this sauce in a large bowl in the microwave while the pasta cooks on the stovetop. Then you can toss the cooked pasta with the sauce without using another bowl - important if you're on clean-up detail!

1 tablespoon	butter	15 mL
1	clove garlic, minced	1
7 or 8	sun-dried tomatoes, cut into thin strips	7 or 8
1/2 cup	whipping cream	125 mL
1 tablespoon	fresh or 1 teaspoon (5 mL) dried basil leaves, crumbled	15 mL
8 ounces	fresh pasta, cooked, drained	250 g
3 tablespoons	minced fresh parsley	50 mL
	Salt and pepper to taste	
	Freshly grated Parmesan cheese	

1. Combine butter and garlic in a large microwave-safe casserole. Microwave on High for 1 1/2 minutes, or until garlic is soft.

2. Add tomatoes, cream and basil. Microwave on Medium for 2 minutes or until hot. Let stand for 5 minutes to soften tomatoes.

3. Cook and drain pasta. Before adding pasta to sauce, reheat sauce if necessary, using Medium power. Add parsley, salt and pepper to taste, then toss pasta and sauce together. Sprinkle with Parmesan and serve at once.

Makes 2 to 4 servings.

Basil

SUN-DRIED TOMATOES

Sun-dried tomatoes can be purchased in bags in specialty food stores, or in the produce departments of many supermarkets. For most recipes, you must soften them before use. Bring 1 cup (250 mL) water to a boil in the microwave. Pour over dried tomatoes and steep for 2 minutes or until soft. Drain, pat dry and use as desired. For the recipe above, the tomatoes can be sliced and used without softening. They will soften in the sauce as it cooks.

BARLEY WITH PINE NUTS

The slightly chewy texture of barley makes this dish an interesting change from potatoes or rice.

1/2 cup	finely chopped celery	125 mL
1/2 cup	chopped onion	125 mL
1 tablespoon	butter	15 mL
1 cup	sliced mushrooms	250 mL
1/4 teaspoon	salt, or to taste	1 mL
1 cup	barley	250 mL
1 3/4 cups	chicken stock	425 mL
1/2 cup	pine nuts	125 mL
1/4 cup	snipped fresh parsley	50 mL
	Dash of pepper	

1. Place celery, onion and butter in an 8-cup (2 L) microwave-safe casserole. Microwave on High for 3 minutes or until vegetables are tender.

2. Stir in mushrooms and microwave on High for 1 minute. Add salt, barley and stock to casserole and stir to mix. Cover casserole and microwave on High for 5 minutes, then on Medium-low for 15 to 17 minutes, or until barley is tender. Add a bit more stock if the mixture is dry and the barley is still too chewy; microwave on Medium-low for a few more minutes.

3. Place pine nuts in a small microwave-safe bowl and microwave on High for 3 to 5 minutes or until nuts are toasted and brown.

4. Stir pine nuts, parsley and pepper into the cooked barley mixture. Taste and adjust seasonings. Serve at once or reheat.

Makes 4 to 6 servings.

Regular Oven Method – BARLEY WITH PINE NUTS

Increase the amount of stock to 2 cups and bake in an uncovered casserole at 350°F (180° C) for 1 hour. Check occasionally and add more stock if the mixture is too dry. Toast pine nuts over low heat in a small, dry skillet.

MICROWAVE HINT – GRAINS

Most grains require little or no stirring during microwave cooking.

TABOULEH SALAD

Bulgur is made from wheat that has been steamed, dried and cracked. For this reason it needs only to be softened with hot water or stock before serving.

1 1/2 cups	water	375 mL
1 cup	bulgur	250 mL
1 1/2 teaspoons	salt	7 mL
3 tablespoons	fresh lemon juice	50 mL
1/2 to 1 teaspoon	minced fresh garlic	2 to 5 mL
1/2 cup	chopped green onion	125 mL
1 1/2 teaspoons	fresh (1/2 teaspoon [2 mL] dried) mint	7 mL
1/4 cup	olive oil	50 mL
	Freshly ground pepper to taste	
2	medium ripe tomatoes, diced	2
1 cup	minced fresh parsley	250 mL

Optional ingredients: cooked chick peas, chopped green pepper, chopped cucumber, grated carrot

1. Pour water into a large microwave-safe bowl or measuring cup and microwave on High for 3 to 5 minutes, or until boiling.

2. Add bulgur and salt and let stand for 20 minutes, or until bulgur is chewable and all water is absorbed.

3. Add lemon juice, garlic, oil and mint and mix well. Refrigerate for 2 to 3 hours to blend flavors.

4. At serving time, add remaining ingredients and mix well. Taste and adjust seasonings. Serve cold. This salad is an excellent side dish for barbecued meat or poultry.

Makes 6 to 8 servings.

PISTACHIO BULGUR PILAF

Bulgur cooks so quickly that it is a great last minute addition to busy weekday dinners. Adding cooked chicken makes it the main course.

1 cup	sliced mushrooms	250 mL
1/2 cup	chopped onion	125 mL
1/2 cup	bulgur	125 mL
2 tablespoons	butter	25 mL
1/2 teaspoon	dried (1 1/2 teaspoons [7 mL] fresh) tarragon leaves	2 mL
1 1/4 cups	chicken stock	300 mL
1/4 cup	coarsely chopped pistachios	50 mL
2 tablespoons	minced fresh parsley	25 mL
1 teapoon	fresh lemon juice	5 mL
	Salt and pepper to taste	

Optional ingredient: 1 cup (250 mL) diced, cooked chicken

1. Place mushrooms, onion, bulgur and butter in an 8-cup (2 L) microwave-safe casserole. Stir to mix well. Microwave on High for 3 minutes or until onion is soft. Stir after 1 minute.

2. Stir in tarragon and stock and microwave on High for 3 minutes, then on Medium-low for 15 minutes or until bulgur is tender and all the liquid is absorbed.

3. Stir in remaining ingredients and season to taste. Serve warm.

Makes 4 servings.

Bulgur Pilaf

This recipe can easily be doubled to accomodate a larger family.

1/4 cup	sliced celery, including leaves	50 mL
1	green onion, chopped	1
2 teaspoons	butter, margarine or oil	10 mL
1/2 cup	bulgur	125 mL
1 cup	chicken stock	250 mL
1/4 teaspoon	salt, or to taste	1 mL
	Freshly ground pepper to taste	
2 tablespoons	chopped pimento or red pepper	25 mL
1 tablespoon	snipped fresh parsley	15 mL

1. Place celery, onion and butter or oil in a 4-cup (1 L) microwave-safe casserole. Microwave on High for 2 minutes, or until vegetables are tender.

2. Stir in bulgur, stock, salt and pepper. Cover and microwave on High for 2 to 4 minutes, or until mixture boils. Stir. Cover and microwave on Low for 10 to 15 minutes, or until liquid is absorbed and bulgur is tender.

3. Stir in pimento or pepper and parsley. Fluff with a fork and serve at once, or keep warm in a 200° F (100° C) oven. Pilaf can also be reheated in the microwave at serving time.

Makes 2 to 3 servings.

Microwave Hint for Seniors or Singles

The microwave is an excellent addition to a senior's or single's kitchen. Small quantities can be prepared quickly and easily, with fewer pots and pans to wash afterwards. Extra portions can be prepared and frozen, to defrost and heat in the microwave at a later date.

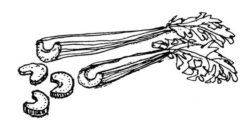

CHEESE POLENTA CASSEROLE

Cook the polenta a day ahead so that it is firm enough to slice to make this dish.

4 cups	water	1 L
2 teaspoons	salt	10 mL
1 1/3 cups	cornmeal	325 mL
2 teaspoons	olive oil	10 mL
1/4 teaspoon	pepper	1 mL
1 1/2 cups	grated mozzarella cheese	375 mL
1/4 cup	grated Parmesan	50 mL

1. Combine water, salt, cornmeal, olive oil and pepper in a large casserole or glass measure. Microwave on High (uncovered) for 12 minutes, or until liquid is absorbed. Stir occasionally. Let stand for 5 minutes. Taste and add more salt and pepper if needed.

2. Spoon polenta into an oiled loaf pan, cool, then cover and refrigerate until cold and firm.

3. Slice cold polenta into 1/2-inch (1 cm) slices. Alternate slices and some of both cheeses in a buttered 9-inch (22 cm)glass pie plate. Sprinkle with paprika. (can cover and refrigerate at this point)

4. Microwave on High for 3 to 5 minutes, or until cheese is melted and bubbly. Serve hot, with your favourite Italian tomato sauce, if desired.

Makes 4 servings.

MICROWAVE HINT

If your microwave is an older model, or if you have noticed that it heats unevenly, be sure to rotate food during cooking to prevent parts of the food from overcooking. This is especially important for foods that are high in fat or sugar and tend to cook quickly.

COUSCOUS WITH SUMMER VEGETABLES

Use the instant variety of couscous when you make this colourful dish.

2 tablespoons	butter	25 mL
1 cup	sliced leeks	250 mL
1 cup	thinly sliced carrots	250 mL
1/2 cup	peas	125 mL
1 1/2 cups	small zucchini chunks	375 mL
1/2 teaspoon	dried oregano (or 2 teaspoons [10 mL] fresh)	2 mL
1 tablespoon	butter (second amount)	15 mL
2 cups	chicken broth	500 mL
1 cup	couscous	250 mL
	Salt and pepper to taste	
2 tablespoons	minced fresh parsley	25 mL

1. Place 2 tablespoons (25 mL) butter, leeks and carrots in a large casserole. Microwave on High for 4 minutes, or until vegetables are crisp-tender. Stir once during cooking.

2. Stir in peas, zucchini and oregano and microwave on High for 2 minutes more. Remove from casserole and set aside.

3. Place 1 tablespoon (15 mL) butter and chicken broth in the casserole. Microwave on High for 5 to 6 minutes, or until broth boils. Stir in couscous, then let stand for 5 minutes, or until couscous absorbs the broth. Fluff couscous with a fork.

4. Toss couscous and vegetables together. Season to taste with salt and pepper. Reheat the mixture, if necessary, on High for a minute or two. Stir in parsley. Spoon into a warm serving dish and serve at once.

Makes 4 to 6 servings.

MICROWAVE HINT – COOKING VEGETABLES

When several vegetables of different densities are cooked together, partially cook the firmer vegetables before adding the softer vegetables that cook more quickly. All vegetables will then finish cooking at the same time.

MILLET AND VEGETABLE PILAF

In the past, we thought of millet only as one of the main ingredients in birdseed. Now many of us are beginning to appreciate its nutritional value as a more complete source of protein than most other grains, and as a source of thiamin, riboflavin, niacin and a fair amount of calcium, magnesium, phosphorus and potassium.

1	large carrot, scrubbed and diced	1
1	medium onion, peeled and chopped	1
1	large rib of celery, sliced	1
1/4 cup	chopped green pepper	50 mL
1/2 teaspoon	dried basil or oregano	2 mL
1 tablespoon	oil	15 mL
1/2 teaspoon	salt, or to taste	2 mL
1 1/4 cups	chicken stock or water	300 mL
1/2 cup	millet	125 mL
1/2 cup	grated cheddar or mozzarella cheese	125 mL
	Freshly ground pepper to taste	
2 tablespoons	fresh minced parsley	25 mL

1. Place vegetables, basil and oil in a large casserole. Add salt and stock or water and stir. Microwave on High for 5 to 7 minutes or until mixture boils.

2. Add millet and stir. Cover and microwave on Medium-low for 20 to 30 minutes or until millet is tender. Add a bit more stock during cooking if the mixture dries out.

3. Stir in cheese, pepper and parsley and more salt if needed. Serve as soon as cheese melts.

Makes 4 servings.

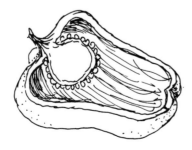

MICROWAVE HINT – PLANNING AHEAD

Cook the rice or grain part of the meal ahead, and reheat in the microwave at serving time. One cup of cooked rice takes about one minute to reheat on High.

CONFETTI RICE RING

This dish serves two purposes in your menu: it is an attractive, colourful and delicious way to serve rice, and the ring itself becomes a serving dish for crisp-tender broccoli, baby carrots, snow peas, or sautéed cherry tomatoes.

3 tablespoons	butter	50 mL
1/2 cup	chopped onion	125 mL
1/4 cup	finely diced carrot	50 mL
1/4 cup	minced sweet red pepper	50 mL
2 1/4 cups	long grain rice	550 mL
4 cups	boiling chicken stock	1 L
3 tablespoons	minced fresh parsley	50 mL
4 teaspoons	butter (second amount)	20 mL
	Salt and pepper to taste	

1. Melt 3 tablespoons (50 mL) butter in a large microwave-safe measuring cup or casserole. Add onion, carrot and red pepper and microwave on High for 4 to 6 minutes, or until vegetables are tender. Stir twice during cooking.

2. Add rice to butter and stir to coat.

3. Stir boiling chicken stock into rice mixture. Cover and microwave on High for 2 minutes, or until stock begins to boil again. Stir. Cover and microwave on Medium-low for 25 minutes, or until rice is tender and liquid is absorbed.

4. Stir in parsley and 4 teaspoons (20 mL) butter. Season to taste with salt and pepper.

5. Generously butter a 6-cup (1.5 L) ring mould. Press rice firmly into the mould. (If not serving at once, cover ring with waxed paper and keep warm.) After one minute, invert the mold onto a serving platter. Carefully remove mould.

6. Fill the center of the rice ring with cooked vegetables of your choice. Broccoli, carrots, snow peas, asparagus or cherry tomatoes work well.

Makes 6 servings.

MICROWAVE HINT

Freeze homemade chicken stock in 2-cup (500 mL) plastic containers to use in your favourite recipes. To defrost, transfer to a 4-cup (1 L) glass measuring cup (unless the plastic container is microwave-safe) and microwave on High for 6 to 8 minutes or until melted.

WILD RICE WITH PECANS

If you wish to keep the cost down, substitute brown rice for half of the wild rice called for in this recipe.

2 tablespoons	butter	25 mL
2 tablespoons	finely diced carrots	25 mL
2 tablespoons	finely diced celery	25 mL
1/4 cup	minced onion	50 mL
1 1/4 cup	wild rice	300 mL
2 cups	hot beef or chicken stock	500 mL
1/2 teaspoon	salt	2 mL
1/2 cup	coarsely chopped pecans	125 mL
2 tablespoons	butter	25 mL
2 tablespoons	minced parsley	25 mL

1. Place butter, carrot, celery and onion in a microwave-safe casserole. Cover and microwave on High for 4 minutes or until vegetables are tender.

2. Add rice and stir to coat with butter. Microwave on High for 2 minutes.

3. Add hot stock and salt. Cover and microwave on High for 3 minutes, or until stock returns to a boil. Reduce power to Low and cook for 30 minutes, or until the rice is tender and all of the stock has been absorbed.

4. Place pecans and butter in a small microwave-safe bowl. Microwave on High for 3 minutes, or until pecans are golden.

5. Stir pecan mixture and minced parsley into cooked rice. Taste and adjust seasonings.

Makes 6 servings

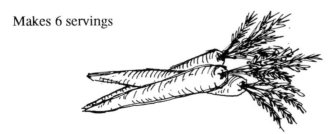

MONEY SAVING TIP

If you buy wild rice at a bulk food store, take a measuring cup along; that way you will be sure to buy only what you need. To maintain freshness, store wild rice in an airtight container.

The Best of
MEAT, FISH, POULTRY & OTHER MAIN DISHES

BEEF STEW WITH HERB DUMPLINGS

Never again will your stew stick to the bottom of the pot
while the dumplings are cooking. Microwave cooking
solves this messy clean-up problem. Stew tastes even
better if made the day before it is served.

Beef Stew:

1 1/2 pounds	beef stew meat, cut into 1-inch (2.5 cm) cubes	750 g
1	package onion soup mix	1
2 1/4 cups	water	550 mL
1/4 cup	dry red wine (or water)	50 mL
2	large potatoes, peeled, cut into 1/2-inch (1 cm) cubes	2
4	carrots, scrubbed, thinly sliced	4
1/4 teaspoon	dried thyme (1 teaspoon [5 mL] fresh)	1 mL
	Freshly ground pepper to taste	
4 tablespoons	cornstarch or commercial gravy maker	50 mL
1/3 cup	cold water	75 mL

1. In a large casserole or microwave simmer pot, mix
together beef, soup mix, water, wine, potatoes, carrots,
thyme and pepper. Stir well. Use the perforated simmer
pot insert or a heatproof plate to submerge the meat and
vegetable chunks under the surface of the stew liquid.
(Floating food pieces dry out and become very hard and
unappetizing.) Cover and microwave on High for 8
minutes, then reduce power level to Low and microwave
for 60 to 90 minutes more, or until the beef is tender.
Remove the plate or insert.

2. In a small bowl combine cornstarch or gravy maker
with cold water. Mix well, then stir into hot stew.
Microwave on High for 3 to 5 minutes, or until thickened.
Stir once. Taste and adjust seasonings.

Makes 6 servings.

HERB DUMPLINGS:

1 1/2 cups	flour	375 mL
1 tablespoon	minced fresh parsley (1 teaspoon [5 mL] dried)	15 mL
1 teaspoon	fresh thyme, rosemary or savory leaves (1/4 teaspoon [1 mL] dried)	5 mL
2 teaspoons	baking powder	10 mL
1/2 teaspoon	salt	2 mL
2/3 cup	milk	150 mL
1	egg	1
2 tablespoons	vegetable oil	25 mL

1. Combine flour, parsley, herbs, baking powder and salt in a small bowl.

2. Combine milk, egg and oil in another small bowl. Add to flour mixture and stir just until blended. Do not overmix or dumplings will be tough.

3. Drop dumplings by spoonfuls onto bubbling stew in a ring around the edge of the casserole. Cover and microwave on High for 5 to 6 minutes, or until dumplings are cooked. Let stand, covered, for 3 minutes before serving.

Makes about 10 dumplings.

MICROWAVE HINTS FOR SOUPS AND STEWS

If you plan to freeze stew, make it without potatoes, as they become mealy after freezing. At serving time, bake 2 potatoes on the microwave, peel and chop them and add to stew.

When you make soup or stew in which pieces of meat or vegetables are cooked in a large amount of liquid, care must be taken to keep pieces submerged in the liquid, as pieces that float on top will overcook and become very hard. Use a heatproof plate or simmer pot insert that fits snugly in the pot, and press it down onto the food until it is totally covered with liquid.

COMPANY COTTAGE CASSEROLE

This is an adaptation of a recipe that my mother-in-law used to make and which my family really enjoys. In our house, it's just called "Casserole."

1 pound	lean ground beef, crumbled	500 g
1 cup	chopped onion	250 mL
1	tin cream of tomato soup	1
2 ounces	cream cheese (1/4 of an 8-ounce [250 g] package)	62.5 g
1/2 teaspoon	salt, or to taste	2 mL
	Freshly ground pepper to taste	
1 teaspoon	Worcestershire sauce	5 mL
1 cup	sliced mushrooms, fresh or canned	250 mL
1/2	of a 12-ounce (350 g) package egg noodles, cooked and drained	1/2
1/2 cup	corn flakes or sliced almonds	125 mL
	Paprika to garnish	

1. Place beef and onion in a large casserole. Cover with casserole lid or waxed paper and microwave on High for 4 to 5 minutes or until beef loses its pink colour and onion is soft. Stir after 2 minutes.

2. Add soup, cheese, salt, pepper, Worcestershire sauce and mushrooms and stir to mix. Microwave on High for 3 minutes, stirring after 2 minutes, until cheese melts and sauce is smooth. Taste and adjust seasonings. Stir in cooked noodles.

3. Pour mixture into an 8-inch (20 cm) round or square baking dish. Sprinkle with cornflakes or almonds (or a combination of both) Sprinkle with paprika.* Microwave on High for 10 minutes or until heated through. If you use a temperature probe, insert it into the center of the casserole and set the probe to 160° F (75° C).

* The casserole can be covered and refrigerated for several hours at this point. Cooking time will be slightly increased if the casserole is cold. It can also be prepared ahead and frozen.

Makes 6 servings.

Regular Oven Method – COMPANY COTTAGE CASSEROLE

Prepare casserole components on stovetop over medium heat. Bake casserole at 275° F (140° C) for 45 minutes, or until heated through.

HAMBURGERS

Sit back and relax, Mom and Dad, and let the children cook these burgers for you tonight. Put your feet up and read the paper, but stay close enough to the kitchen to offer technical advice or help, if needed.

1 pound	lean ground beef	500 g
1/4 cup	finely chopped onion	50 mL
1 teaspoon	salt	5 mL
1/4 teaspoon	pepper	1 mL
1 tablespoon	barbecue sauce or ketchup	15 mL
4	slices of cheese (optional)	4
4	hamburger buns	4
	Mustard, relish, ketchup, sliced tomatoes, pickle slices, or whatever you like on your hamburgers	

1. Combine beef, onion, salt, pepper and barbecue sauce or ketchup in a medium bowl. Use a spoon or your (clean) hands to mix the ingredients well. Divide the mixture into 4 equal pieces and shape each piece into a patty.

2. Place patties on a microwave-safe tray or baking pan and cover with waxed paper. Microwave on High for 2 minutes. Turn patties over and microwave on High for 3 more minutes. If you like your burgers well done, microwave on High for one minute more.

3. If cheeseburgers are desired, top patties with cheese and let stand for 2 minutes. If the cheese isn't melted after standing time, microwave on High for 20 seconds more.

4. To warm buns: Put buns on a plate and cover with a paper towel or clean tea towel. Microwave on High for 45 seconds to 1 minute, or until buns are hot.

Makes 4 servings.

MICROWAVE HINT

Before you store your barbecue for the winter, grill and freeze a supply of beef patties, pork chops, ribs and chicken pieces. When you reheat them in the microwave, they will taste freshly grilled.

LASAGNE

The most tedious part of making lasagne – cooking the noodles – has been eliminated in this microwave version of a family favourite. Read the helpful hints at the end of the recipe for best results.

l pound	hot or sweet Italian sausage, crumbled	500 g
1	clove garlic, minced	1
2 teaspoons	dried crumbled basil leaves	10 mL
l teaspoon	salt	5 mL
3 1/2 cups	canned tomatoes,including liquid,chopped	875 mL
1	tin tomato paste, 5 1/2 oz.(156 mL)	1
l pound	ricotta cheese	500 g
3	eggs, beaten	3
2 tablespoons	minced fresh parsley	25 mL
l/2 cup	grated Parmesan or romano cheese	125 mL
l teaspoon	salt (second amount)	5 mL
l/2 teaspoon	pepper	2 mL
3 cups	shredded mozzarella cheese, about 12 ounces (350 g)	750 mL
8 to 10	uncooked lasagne noodles	8 to 10
2 tablespoons	grated Parmesan (second amount)	25 mL

1. Place meat and garlic in a large casserole. Cover and microwave on High for 4 to 5 minutes, or until completely browned. Stir once during cooking. Drain excess fat.

2. Add basil, salt, tomatoes and tomato paste to meat. Cover and microwave on High for 5 minutes. Set aside.

3. In a large bowl, combine ricotta, eggs, parsley, 1/2 cup (125 mL) Parmesan, 1 teaspoon salt and pepper. Set aside.

4. Layer the assembled ingredients in a 13 x 9-inch (34 by 22 cm)glass baking dish, or the largest flat 2 quart (2 L) casserole you can fit in your microwave, in the following order:

- 1 cup (250 mL) meat sauce, evenly spread

Regular Oven Method – LASAGNE

Cook and drain lasagna noodles. Layer in 13 X 9-inch (34 by 22 cm) pan in this order: 5 noodles, half ricotta filling, half mozzarella, half meat sauce, remaining noodles, remaining ricotta, half remaining mozzarella, remaining meat sauce, remaining mozzarella, 2 tablespoons (25 mL) Parmesan. Bake at 375° F (190° C) for 30 minutes. Let stand 10 minutes before cutting.

- 4 or 5 uncooked noodles, overlapped slightly if necessary
- 1 cup (250 mL) meat sauce
- half of the ricotta mixture
- half of the mozzarella
- 1 cup (250 mL) meat sauce
- remaining noodles
- remaining mozzarella
- remaining meat sauce
- remaining ricotta mixture

5. Cover with microwave-safe plastic wrap and microwave on High for 15 minutes. If cooking seems to be uneven, rotate the dish halfway through cooking.

6. Reduce power to Medium-low and microwave for 20 to 25 minutes, or until noodles are tender. Sprinkle with 2 tablespoons (25 mL) Parmesan and microwave on High (uncovered) for 1 minute, or until cheese melts. Let stand, covered, for 10 minutes before serving.

Makes 6 servings.

COOKING TIPS FOR PERFECT MICROWAVE LASAGNE

You should have about 4 cups (1 L) of tomato sauce for 10 lasagne noodles to provide enough liquid to sufficiently soften the uncooked noodles.

The mozzarella cheese must be under the sauce rather than on top of the casserole to prevent the cooked cheese from overcooking and becoming tough.
If ricotta cheese is unavailable in your area, substitute small-curd, cream-style cottage cheese. Lean ground beef can replace the Italian sausage.

Elevating the baking pan one inch (2 cm) in your microwave will enable the food to cook more evenly. I place my bacon rack in the microwave to elevate the pan, but an inverted, microwave-safe plate can be used as well.

Since a large rectangular pan will not fit in my microwave because of the turntable, I have successfully made lasagne in a large simmer pot or Dutch oven. It looks a little different but tastes the same.

MICROWAVE CHILI

If your family doesn't like kidney beans, substitute a 19-ounce(540 mL) tin of baked beans. Serve on rice, if desired.

1 1/2 pounds	lean ground beef, crumbled	750 g
1 cup	chopped onion	250 mL
1/2 cup	chopped green pepper	125 mL
1/4 cup	chopped celery	50 mL
2	cloves garlic, minced	2
3 cups	canned tomatoes, broken up	750 mL
1	7 1/2-ounce (213 mL) tin tomato sauce	1
4 teaspoons	chili powder, or to taste	20 mL
1/4 teaspoon	crushed dried chilies, or to taste	1 mL
1/2 teaspoon	ground cumin	2 mL
1/2 teaspoon	dried oregano	2 mL
1	19-ounce (540 mL) tin red kidney beans, drained	1
	Salt and pepper to taste	
	Grated cheddar cheese to garnish	

1. Combine beef, onion, green pepper, celery and garlic in a large microwave-safe casserole. Cover loosely with plastic wrap or casserole lid and microwave on High for 8 to 10 minutes or until meat is no longer pink. Stir after 4 and 8 minutes. Pour off excess fat.

2. Add tomatoes, tomato sauce, chili powder, dried chilies, cumin and oregano to beef mixture. Cover and microwave on High for 10 minutes, stirring once after 5 minutes.

3. Add kidney beans. Microwave on High for 5 minutes more. Season to taste with salt and pepper, and with more chili powder and dried chilies if desired. Sprinkle each serving with grated cheese.

Makes 6 servings.

MICROWAVE HINT – COOKING GROUND BEEF

To reduce fat when cooking ground beef in the microwave, crumble beef into a microwave-safe colander set over a drip-catching pan. Microwave on High until beef is no longer pink, then transfer to microwave-safe casserole and continue recipe. Discard fat that has accumulated in the pan beneath.

Sweet and Sour Meatballs

Cooked rice freezes well, so make extra to have ready when you serve these meatballs.

2 pounds	lean ground beef	1 kg
2	eggs	2
1 1/2 teaspoons	salt	7 mL
1/2 teaspoon	pepper	2 mL
2/3 cup	finely minced onion	150 mL
2	cloves garlic, minced	2
1/3 cup	dry breadcrumbs	75 mL
1/2 cup	vinegar	125 mL
1/2 cup	brown sugar	125 mL
1/3 cup	ketchup	75 mL
2 tablespoons	soy sauce	25 mL
2 tablespoons	cornstarch	25 mL
1	tin (19 ounces [540 mL]) pineapple chunks, drained, juice reserved	1
1 cup	sliced green pepper	250 mL

1. Combine beef, eggs, salt, pepper, onion, garlic and breadcrumbs. Shape into 48 meatballs and place half of the balls in a microwave-safe baking dish. Cover with waxed paper and microwave on High for 4 minutes.

2. Rotate and rearrange meatballs so that those that are less cooked are close to the outer edge of the dish. Cover and microwave on High for 4 to 6 more minutes, or until meatballs are cooked through and firm to the touch. Drain off excess fat and set meatballs aside, discard fat. Repeat with remaining meatballs.

3. Place vinegar, brown sugar, ketchup, soy sauce, cornstarch and reserved pineapple juice in a 4-cup (1 L) glass measure. Microwave on High for 5 minutes, or until thickened. Stir once.

4. Stir in pineapple and green pepper. Gently combine meatballs and sauce in a large microwave-safe casserole. Cover and microwave on High for 3 to 5 minutes, stirring occasionally, until meatballs are heated through. Serve on hot rice, or on toothpicks as appetizers.

Makes 8 servings.

Microwave Hint – Meatballs

Meatballs can be cooked as above and frozen without sauce. For a quick meal, defrost and mix with your favourite Italian tomato sauce, cream of mushroom soup, cheese sauce, etc., and serve over hot pasta, rice or mashed potatoes.

Moussaka

Moussaka is an excellent choice when you're entertaining. It can be prepared the day before, or can be made ahead and frozen. *Harrowsmith* cookbook editors liked my version so much that they departed from their "no microwave recipes" tradition and published this recipe in their "Simmering Suppers" cookbook.

Eggplant Layer:

2	medium eggplants, about 1 pound (500 gm) each Salt	2

1. Peel eggplant and cut into slices 1/2-inch (1 cm) thick. Sprinkle slices lightly with salt, set on paper towels, cover with a layer of paper towels and a heavy tray to weight the slices down, and let stand for 1/2 hour.

2. Pat eggplant slices dry. Arrange in a circle around the edge of a heatproof plate. Cover with plastic wrap and microwave on High for 4 to 6 minutes or until cooked. Repeat until all eggplant slices are cooked.

3. Place half of the eggplant slices in an overlapping layer in a rectangular glass baking dish that is 8 x 10 x 2-inches (3 L capacity). Set remaining eggplant aside.

Filling:

2 tablespoons	oil	25 mL
2/3 cup	chopped onion	150 mL
1 1/3 pounds	lean ground lamb or beef	650 g
1 cup	chopped tomatoes	250 mL
1	5 1/2-ounce (156 mL) tin tomato paste	1
1	clove garlic, minced	1
1 teaspoon	dried oregano leaves	5 mL
1/2 teaspoon	cinnamon	2 mL
	Salt and freshly ground pepper to taste	
6 tablespoons	Parmesan cheese	100 mL

1. Place oil and onion in a large casserole. Microwave on High for 3 minutes or until onion is soft. Stir in meat. Cover and microwave on High for 5 to 6 minutes, or until no pink colour is visible in the meat. Stir twice during cooking.

Regular Oven Method – Moussaka

Fry eggplant slices in skillet on stove in a small amount of oil until lightly browned and soft. Drain on paper towels.Make filling and bechamel in pot on stove. Assemble Moussaka as above, and bake at 325° F (160° C) for 30 minutes, then 400° F (200° C) for 10 minutes, or until brown and bubbly.

2. Add tomatoes, paste, garlic, oregano and cinnamon. Microwave on High, uncovered, for 7 minutes or until filling is thick and most of the moisture has evaporated. (Cooking the filling on the stove over medium heat will take about 20 minutes.) Stir occasionally during cooking.

3. Season filling to taste with salt and pepper. Spread evenly over the eggplant layer in the baking pan and sprinkle with 2 tablespoons (25 mL) Parmesan. Layer remaining eggplant slices over the filling and sprinkle with 2 more tablespoons (25 mL) Parmesan.

BECHAMEL SAUCE:

1 1/3 cups	milk	325 mL
2 teaspoons	butter	10 mL
2	eggs	2
3 tablespoons	flour	50 mL
1/4 teaspoon	salt	1 mL

1. Heat 1 cup (250 mL) milk and butter in a 4-cup (1 L) glass measure on Medium for 2 minutes or until scalded (150° F [70° C] on probe).

2. Whisk remaining milk, eggs, flour and salt in a medium bowl. Slowly whisk hot milk into egg mixture. Pour the mixture back into measuring cup and microwave on Medium for 3 minutes or until thick. Whisk several times during cooking.

3. Pour bechamel sauce over the top eggplant layer in baking pan and sprinkle with remaining 2 tablespoons (25 mL) Parmesan and a bit of paprika. Microwave on High for 20 to 25 minutes, or until Moussaka is hot and bubbly. Let stand for 10 minutes before serving.

Makes 6 servings.

DEFROSTING IN THE MICROWAVE

Foods that are more dense (such as roasts or casseroles) take longer to defrost than less dense foods such as bread or pastry.

SALISBURY STEAK

I developed this recipe in answer to a reader request. I have heard from a neighbour since that her children, normally picky eaters, really enjoy this tasty main dish. If you don't have a browning dish, brown patties on stovetop, then transfer to microwave to finish cooking.

1 pound	lean ground beef	500 g
1/2 cup	finely chopped onion	125 mL
1 tablespoon	minced fresh parsley	15 mL
1	clove garlic, minced	1
1	egg	1
1/4 cup	fine breadcrumbs	50 mL
2 tablespoons	ketchup or tomato sauce	25 mL
1/2 teaspoon	Worcestershire sauce	2 mL
1/2 teaspoon	salt	2 mL
1/2 teaspoon	dried thyme	2 mL
1/4 teaspoon	pepper	1 mL
2 tablespoons	oil	25 mL
1 cup	sliced fresh mushrooms	250 mL
1/3 cup	chopped onion (second amount)	75 mL
1 1/4 cups	beef broth	300 mL
2 tablespoons	cornstarch	25 mL
	Salt and pepper to taste	
	minced fresh parsley	

1. Combine beef, 1/2 cup (125 mL) onion, parsley, garlic, egg, breadcrumbs, ketchup, Worcestershire, salt, thyme and pepper. Mix well. Shape into 4 patties the same size and shape.

2. Preheat a browning dish, then add oil. Place patties in browning dish, pressing so that the entire patty is in contact with the surface of the dish. Brown for 1 minute, then turn patties over. Microwave on High for 3 minutes, then transfer patties to a plate. Patties can also be browned in a skillet on the stovetop.

3. Place mushrooms and onions in the same browning dish and microwave on High for 2 to 3 minutes or until onions are soft.

4. Stir cornstarch into beef broth, then stir this mixture slowly into the mushroom mixture. Microwave on High for 3 to 4 minutes, or until the gravy is thickened. Stir several times during cooking to prevent gravy from becoming lumpy. A whisk works best for this. Add salt and pepper to taste.

5. Return patties to pan and spoon gravy over them. Cover pan with waxed paper or lid and microwave on Medium for 10 minutes, or until patties are cooked through. If gravy thickens too much during cooking, whisk in a bit more beef broth until desired consistency is achieved.

6. Serve patties and gravy with potatoes, pasta or rice. Sprinkle each serving with minced fresh parsley.

Makes 4 servings.

MICROWAVE HINT – USING A BROWNING DISH

Browning dishes must be preheated before food is added, or food will not brown. You must press the food to make contact with the surface of the dish: only parts of the food that are touching the hot dish will brown.

Pork Tenderloins stuffed with Pistachios and Fruit

Serve this main course the next time you entertain. It is very attractive when sliced.

2	large pork tenderloins	2
16	slices bacon	16
2/3 cup	diced onion	150 mL
2	apples, peeled, cored, diced	2
2/3 cup	shelled pistachios (see note)	150 mL
1/4 cup	chopped dried apricots	50 mL
1/4 cup	raisins	50 mL
1/4 teaspoon	dried sage	1 mL
1 to 1 1/2 cups	dry breadcrumbs	250 to 375 mL
1/2 cup	chicken stock or water, or enough to moisten	125 mL
	Salt and pepper to taste	

Note: Other nuts such as walnuts, pecans or hazelnuts can replace the pistachios, but the colour of the pistachios in the finished dish is especially attractive.

1. Butterfly each tenderloin; open flat and place between 2 sheets of plastic wrap. Pound with a rolling pin until meat is 1/2-inch (1 cm) thick. Set aside.

2. Chop 4 slices of bacon into 1-inch (2.5 cm) pieces and place in a medium casserole along with onion. Microwave on High for 3 to 5 minutes, or until onion is soft. Stir twice during cooking. Add apples, pistachios, apricots, raisins, sage and breadcumbs and stir to mix well. Add enough stock to moisten the stuffing so that it will hold together. Add salt and pepper to taste.

3. Spoon half of the stuffing along the center of each tenderloin. Pull the edges of the meat up to cover the stuffing. Meat at this point is log-shaped.

4. Wrap 6 slices of bacon around each tenderloin and tie a piece of string to secure each slice of bacon.

5. Place 1 tenderloin seam side down on a microwave-safe baking pan. Microwave on Medium for 15 minutes. Wrap

Regular Oven Method – PORK TENDERLOIN STUFFED WITH PISTACHIOS AND FRUIT

Prepare filling on stovetop in large pot. Roast tenderloins at 325° F (160° C) for 45 minutes to 1 hour, or until pork is completely cooked.

ends of the meat roll in foil. Microwave on Medium for 5 to 10 minutes more, or until a sharp knife blade inserted into the center of the meat for 10 seconds feels hot to the touch.

6. Repeat cooking procedure with other tenderloin.

7. Cool tenderloins for 10 minutes before slicing, or cook, wrap well and refrigerate until serving time (can also be cooked and frozen).

8. To reheat, arrange 6 to 8 slices in a circle on a microwave-safe plate, cover and microwave on High for 1 minute or until heated through. Transfer to a serving platter and garnish with parsley and cherry tomatoes.

Makes 6 servings.

MICROWAVE HINT – REHEATING

It is difficult to heat a large mass of food to the center without overcooking the outside. For this reason, it is better to reheat individual servings rather than the whole casserole or roast. Smaller quantities will heat quickly, and will have better flavour and texture.

PORK MEDALLIONS IN ROQUEFORT CREAM SAUCE

This recipe by Barb Holland and Roxanne McQuilkin is from their cookbook, *Microwave Cooking With Style*, one of the best books available for entertaining recipes for the microwave.

2 tablespoons	vegetable oil	25 mL
1 1/2 pounds	pork tenderloin, cut into 1/2-inch (1 cm) slices	750 g
2 tablespoons	butter	25 mL
1	onion, chopped	1
1 cup	sliced mushrooms	250 mL
2 tablespoons	all-purpose flour	25 mL
1/2 teaspoons	salt	2 mL
1/2 teaspoon	ground cumin	2 mL
1/4 teaspoon	freshly ground pepper	1 mL
1/2 cup	dry vermouth or white wine	125 mL
1/2 cup	chicken stock	125 mL
1/4 cup	crumbled Roquefort or blue cheese	50 mL
1/2 cup	plain yogurt or sour cream	125 mL

1. Heat oil in a large skillet on stove top. Quickly sauté pork slices on both sides until lightly browned. Remove with a slotted spoon and set aside. Cook in batches if necessary.

2. In an 8-cup (2 L) microwave-safe casserole, combine butter, onion and mushrooms. Microwave, uncovered, on High for 2 to 3 minutes, or until softened. Stir in flour, salt, cumin and pepper and microwave on High for 1 minute. Whisk in vermouth and chicken stock. Cover and microwave on High for 2 to 3 minutes, or until sauce boils.

3. Stir in pork slices, cover and microwave on High for 5 minutes. Stir, cover and microwave on Medium for 10 to 15 minutes, or until pork is tender and no longer pink in the center.

4. Stir in cheese, mashing to blend with hot sauce. Stir in yogurt or sour cream. Microwave on Medium-high for 2 to 3 minutes, or until just heated through. Do not boil.

5. Serve over cooked noodles or rice.

Makes 6 servings.

ITALIAN PORK CHOP CASSEROLE

I always demonstrate this easy and delicious recipe in my microwave cooking classes. You can substitute boneless chicken breast halves, veal chops or thinly sliced round steak for the pork chops.

4	pork loin chops	4
1 tablespoons	vegetable oil	15 mL
2 cups	your favourite Italian tomato sauce	500 mL
4	slices mozzarella cheese	4
1/4 cup	freshly grated Parmesan cheese	50 mL
4	servings of hot cooked pasta	4

1. Coat bottom and sides of an 8 or 9-inch (20 - 22 cm) microwave-safe baking dish with the oil. Arrange the chops on the oil, with the bone facing the center of the dish, leaving the center of the dish empty to ensure even cooking. Top each chop with a slice of mozzarella and pour the sauce over all. Sprinkle with Parmesan.

2. Cover pan with plastic wrap or a lid, and microwave on High for 5 minutes, then Medium for 10 to 15 minutes, or until the chops are tender and cooked through. Serve with hot cooked pasta and more Parmesan.

Makes 4 servings.

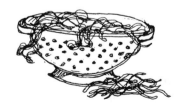

Satay With Peanut Sauce

Satay is usually grilled or broiled, but it can be cooked in the microwave. Serve it with with steamed rice and a cool cucumber salad to contrast the exotic, spicy flavors of the Peanut Sauce.

1/2 cup	soy sauce	125 mL
1/4 cup	dry sherry	50 mL
1 tablespoon	brown sugar	15 mL
2	cloves garlic, minced	2
1 1/2 pounds	lean boneless pork or chicken breast meat, in 1-inch (2.5 cm) cubes	750 g

1. Combine soy sauce, sherry, sugar and garlic in a bowl. Add pork and marinate at room temperature for 1/2 hour.

2. Remove meat from marinade and thread onto bamboo skewers. To cook in the microwave, arrange skewers in a spoke pattern on a microwave-safe plate. Brush with marinade and cover with waxed paper. Microwave on High for 5 minutes. Rotate the skewers end to end, brush with marinade and cover with waxed paper. Microwave on High for 5 minutes more, or until pork is thoroughly cooked. If you prefer, broil or grill over hot coals for 15 to 20 minutes, turning occasionally, until meat is cooked. If chicken is used, decrease cooking time to 10 minutes.

3. Serve Satay with Peanut Sauce (recipe follows) either hot or at room temperature, garnished with fresh coriander sprigs.

Makes 4 to 6 servings.

Microwave Hint

Foods that are best served at room temperature can be warmed slightly in the microwave using Defrost. Time required will vary with quantity, so check often and be careful not to overheat.

Peanut Sauce

You may wish to decrease the red pepper flakes, as this sauce is quite spicy.

1	green onion, minced	1
3	cloves garlic, crushed	3
1/2 teaspoon	crushed dried red pepper flakes, or to taste	2 mL
1/4 teaspoon	ground coriander	1 mL
3/4 to 1 cup	coconut milk (see note)	175 to 250 mL
2 teaspoons	brown sugar	10 mL
1/4 cup	crunchy peanut butter	50 mL

Note: You can make your own coconut milk by squeezing the juice from freshly grated coconut, or you can purchase creamed coconut in a solid block in many produce or specialty food shops. The recipe for reconstituting this product is on the back of the box.

1. Purée onion, garlic, red pepper and coriander in a blender or food processor until finely chopped.

2. Transfer to a glass measuring cup or heatproof bowl and microwave on High for 2 minutes, stirring occasionally. Whisk in coconut milk, then stir in brown sugar and peanut butter. Microwave on High for 1 minute. Stir until smooth. If mixture is too thick for dipping, add more coconut milk.

3. Refrigerate until serving time, then serve at room temperature with Satay. Peanut Sauce can be made up to 3 days ahead. Store in the refrigerator.

Makes about 1 cup (250 mL).

CRAB STUFFED SOLE

Beautiful, delicious and low in calories when made with yogurt rather than sour cream. These rolls can be assembled several hours ahead, refrigerated, and cooked in the microwave just before serving.

1	5 1/2-ounce (156 mL) tin crabmeat	1
2	green onions, chopped	2
1/3 cup	minced sweet red pepper	75 mL
2 to 3 tablespoons	sour cream or plain yogurt	25 to 45 mL
2 teaspoons	fresh lemon juice	10 mL
1 teaspoon	Dijon mustard	5 mL
2 tablespoons	minced fresh dill	25 mL
1 tablespoon	minced fresh parsley	15 mL
	Salt and pepper to taste	
8	small sole fillets, 2 ounces (65 g) each	8
1/4 cup	white wine or water	50 mL

1. Drain crabmeat and remove any bits of shell or cartilage. Place in a small bowl and mix with onion, red pepper, 2 tablespoons (25 mL) sour cream or yogurt, lemon juice, mustard, dill and parsley. Add more sour cream or yogurt if the mixture is not moist enough. Season to taste with pepper and salt and more dill and parsley if desired.

2. Spread 1/8 of the filling on each sole fillet and roll up like a jelly roll. Secure each roll with a toothpick.

3. Arrange rolls standing on end or seam side down in a circle in a 10-inch (24 cm) round glass baking dish. Pour wine around rolls. Cover dish with waxed paper and microwave on High for 6 to 8 minutes. Partway through cooking, rotate rolls, placing the less cooked part to face the edge of the dish. The fish is cooked when it flakes easily with a fork.

4. Carefully remove toothpicks and transfer rolls to a warm platter. Garnish with parsley, dill sprigs and lemon wedges.

Makes 4 servings.

MICROWAVE HINT – ELIMINATING "FISHY" ODOURS

To remove unpleasant smells from your microwave, place a lemon slice in a cup half-full of water. Microwave on High for 5 minutes, then leave in microwave for 2 minutes more. Wipe out oven.

FISH FILLETS WITH VEGETABLES

Serve rice or pasta to accompany this healthy, low-fat dish. I have also enjoyed it with good rye bread (no butter) to soak up the delicious juice.

1 cup	tomato juice	250 mL
3 tablespoons	fresh lemon juice	50 mL
2	carrots, peeled, in thin julienne strips	2
1	stalk celery, in thin diagonal slices	1
1/4 cup	finely chopped onion	50 mL
2 tablespoons	minced parsley	25 mL
1/2 teaspoon	dried oregano or thyme	2 mL
1/4 teaspoon	pepper	1 mL
1 pound	fish fillets (sole or haddock, or your favourite)	500 g
4 teaspoons	Parmesan cheese	20 mL

1. Combine all ingredients except fish in an 8-inch (20 cm) baking dish. Microwave on High for 9 minutes, or until carrots are just tender and liquid is boiling. Stir twice.

2. Arrange fillets on top of the vegetable mixture in a circle with the thickest part of the fillet facing the outside edge of the dish. Spoon some of the vegetable mixture over the fillets. Sprinkle with Parmesan.

3. Cover dish with plastic wrap and microwave on High for 3 to 4 minutes, or until fish is opaque and flakes easily with a fork.

4. Spoon some sauce over each serving. Accompany the fish with rice or plain pasta.

Makes 4 servings.

FOR TWO SERVINGS:

Cut the quantity of all ingredients in half and cut cooking time to about 6 minutes before the fish is added. After adding fish, microwave on High for 2 minutes. Check for doneness, and cook longer, if necessary.

MICROWAVE HINT

When cooking fish, it is important for best flavour and texture not to overcook it. Check halfway through cooking time, and again two minutes before the cooking time is up. Remember that some cooking will occur during standing time.

DILLED SALMON MOUSSE

This mousse is perfect for entertaining, because it can be made a day ahead. Serve it as an appetizer spread with cucumber slices or crackers, or as a luncheon or light supper entrée.

1 pound	fresh salmon or 2 tins red salmon (7 1/2 ounces [213 g] each)	500 g
1 teaspoon	lemon juice	5 mL
1	envelope gelatin (1 tablespoon [15 mL])	1
1/4 cup	cold water	50 mL
1/2 cup	water (second amount)	125 mL
1/2 cup	mayonnaise	125 mL
1/4 cup	snipped fresh dill	50 mL
1 tablespoon	lemon juice	15 mL
1 tablespoon	minced fresh chives	15 mL
1/4 teaspoon	hot pepper sauce, or to taste	1 mL
1/2 cup	whipping cream, whipped	125 mL
1/2 teaspoon	salt	2 mL
	Freshly ground pepper to taste	

1. To cook fresh salmon: Place salmon pieces in a shallow microwave-safe dish. Sprinkle 1 teaspoon (5 mL) lemon juice over. Cover with plastic wrap and microwave on Medium for 5 minutes. Rearrange pieces, cover and microwave on Medium for 3 to 5 minutes more, or until salmon is opaque and flakes easily with a fork. Cool, then remove skin and bones and mince salmon with a fork. Refrigerate until needed. If you are using canned salmon, drain it, remove skin and bones and mince with a fork. Stir in lemon juice. Refrigerate until needed.

2. Sprinkle gelatin over cold water in a small glass bowl. Let stand for 5 minutes to soften.

3. Bring 1/2 cup (125 mL) water to a boil in the microwave. Stir into softened gelatin until the gelatin dissolves. Cool for 5 minutes, then add mayonnaise, dill, lemon juice, chives and hot pepper sauce. Refrigerate for 15 to 20 minutes, or until the mixture is the consistency of unbeaten egg white. Check every 5 minutes.

Chives

4. Stir salmon into the thickened gelatin mixture. Fold in the whipped cream and season to taste with salt, pepper and more dill if desired.

5. Pour mixture into a well-oiled 4-cup (1 L) mould, cover with plastic wrap and refrigerate 4 hours or overnight.

6. Dip mould into hot water at serving time to make unmoulding easier. Wipe mould dry, then invert onto serving platter. Garnish with parsley, cucumber slices and cherry tomatoes.

Makes 6 to 8 servings.

MICROWAVE HINT – FRESH DILL

Many herbs dry well in the microwave, but dill isn't one of them. To best preserve the flavour, freeze snipped fresh dill. I keep it in a jar on the door of my freezer, ready to scoop out as needed.

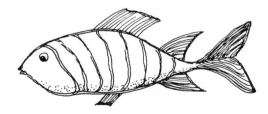

PARMESAN SOLE

This recipe can also be cooked in a hot oven, but the microwave version is faster and more moist.

3 tablespoons	chopped parsley	50 mL
3 tablespoons	minced onion	50 mL
4	sole fillets, fresh or defrosted	
1 tablespoon	fresh lemon juice	15 mL
3 to 4 tablespoons	freshly grated Parmesan cheese	50 mL
	Freshly ground pepper	
	Paprika	
	Lemon wedges and parsley to garnish	

1. Sprinkle parsley and onion on the bottom of an 8 or 9-inch (20 - 22 cm) microwave-safe pan. Place fillets on the parsley mixture, arranging them around the outside edge of the dish with the thickest part of the fish near the edge of the dish.

2. Sprinkle fillets with lemon juice, pepper, Parmesan and paprika. Cover the dish with waxed paper and microwave on High for 4 minutes. Check the thickest part for doneness. If not cooked through (fish will be opaque and will flake easily with a fork if it is cooked) continue cooking on High, testing every 30 seconds.

3. Let stand, covered, for 2 minutes. Garnish and serve.

Makes 4 servings.

Regular Oven Method – PARMESAN SOLE

Prepare as above and broil 6 inches from element until cheese melts and fish flakes.

MICROWAVE HINT – COOKING FISH

For even cooking and best results, completely defrost fish before cooking in the microwave.

SHRIMP AND CHICKEN CREOLE

This interesting mixture of chicken and seafood from Anne Lindsay's *Lighthearted Cookbook* is not only lovely to look at and taste, it is also heart-healthy. I have adapted it to microwave cooking.

1 1/2 pounds	boneless chicken cut into bitesize pieces	750 g
1 tablespoon	vegetable oil	15 mL
2	onions, coarsely chopped	2
3	cloves garlic, minced	3
1	each, sweet red and green pepper, coarsely chopped	1
1	28-ounce (796 mL) tin tomatoes, undrained, chopped	1
4 cups	chicken stock	1 L
1 teaspoon	dried thyme	5 mL
1 teaspoon	dried oregano	5 mL
1/4 teaspoon	cayenne pepper	1 mL
2 cups	parboiled (converted) rice	500 mL
1 pound	medium shrimp (fresh or frozen)	500 g
1/2 cup	chopped fresh parsley	125 mL

1. Place chicken, oil, onion and garlic in a large microwave-safe casserole. Microwave on High for 8 to 9 minutes, or until vegetables are soft and chicken is no longer pink. Stir every two minutes during cooking.

2. Stir in peppers, tomatoes, stock and spices. Microwave on High for 8 minutes or until boiling.

3. Stir in rice. Cover and microwave on Medium-low for 30 to 35 minutes, or until rice is tender and some of the liquid is absorbed. Stir after 10 minutes.

4. Place shrimp in a microwave-safe casserole and microwave on High, covered, for about 3 minutes. Check after 1 1/2 minutes and remove the shrimps that have turned pink. Continue to cook, checking every 30 seconds, and removing the shrimp that have turned pink. Do not overcook or the shrimp will be tough.

5. Shell and devein shrimp, then stir them into the Creole mixture. Microwave on High for 3 minutes, or until heated through. Stir in parsley.

Makes 8 servings.

MICROWAVE HINT

Large and medium shrimp require the same amount of cooking time in the microwave for the same quantity. Cover the dish tightly with plastic wrap or lid during cooking. Rearrange shrimp during cooking and remove any that have finished cooking. Do not overcook, or shrimp will be tough.

CHICKEN AND VEGETABLE FRIED RICE

Don't worry if you're missing some of the vegetables listed in this recipe. Use any vegetables you have on hand, in whatever quantities you like. Try to have a variety of colours, if possible.

2 tablespoons	vegetable oil	25 mL
1/2 cup	chopped onion	125 mL
1	clove garlic, minced	1
1/2 cup	thinly sliced carrots	125 mL
1/2 cup	thinly sliced celery	125 mL
1/2 cup	chopped red or green pepper (or some of both)	125 mL
1/2 cup	snow peas, broccoli florets or defrosted peas	125 mL
1 cup	sliced mushrooms	250 mL
1 to 2 cups	chopped cooked chicken	250 to 500 mL
3 cups	cold cooked rice	750 mL
	Soy sauce to taste	
1/4 cup	minced fresh parsley	50 mL

1. Place oil, onion and garlic in a large microwave-safe casserole. Microwave on High for 3 minutes or until onion is soft. Stir once.

2. Add carrots, celery, pepper, peas or broccoli and mushrooms. Microwave on High for 5 minutes, or until vegetables are crisp-tender. Stir several times during cooking.

3. Stir in chicken and rice and two tablespoons soy sauce. Cover and microwave on High for 5 minutes, or until mixture is very hot. Stir occasionally. Taste and add more soy sauce and salt and pepper as needed. Stir in parsley and serve at once.

Makes 4 to 6 servings.

COOKING TIP – CREATIVE COOKING WITH CHILDREN

If a tour of your refrigerator reveals leftover rice, cooked chicken and a few vegetables, why not invite your child to help you create a tasty one-dish microwave meal for the whole family to enjoy? This type of cooking shows children how important it is not to waste leftover food. Most children enjoy eating their own cooking, even when a dish contains foods they normally don't enjoy.

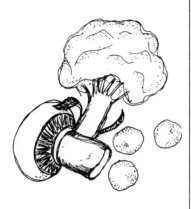

CHICKEN AND VEGETABLE STIR FRY

This is another good recipe to use up the little bits of vegetables that accumulate in your crisper over the week.

1/2	chicken breast, cut into bitesize pieces	.5
1/2 teaspoon	cornstarch	2 mL
	Dash of garlic powder and soy sauce	
	Dash of salt and pepper	
1 tablespoon	oil	15 mL
2 cups	your choice of thinly sliced vegetables: broccoli, mushrooms, celery, onions, carrots, peas, green or red pepper, bean sprouts, etc.	500 mL

1. Place chicken pieces in a small bowl. Combine cornstarch, garlic powder, soy sauce, salt and pepper and toss with chicken.

2. Pour oil into a 6 to 8-cup (1.5 to 2 L) microwave-safe casserole. Add firm vegetables such as onions, carrots and celery. Microwave on High for 2 minutes, or until vegetables are crisp-tender.

3. Stir in chicken and remaining vegetables; stir to coat pieces with oil. Microwave on High for 3 to 5 minutes, or until chicken is cooked through (cut a large piece in half: it should be white all the way through) and vegetables are cooked to desired degree of doneness.

4. Serve on hot cooked rice, or with Bulgur Pilaf.

Makes 2 servings.

CORNISH HENS WITH WILD RICE

A lovely entrée for an intimate dinner for two.

2	small (1 pound [500 g] or less) Cornish hens	2
2 teaspoons	butter	10 mL
1	green onion, chopped	1
1 cup	cooked wild rice	250 mL
1/2 teaspoon	fresh thyme leaves	2 mL
1/4 cup	coarsely chopped pecans	50 mL
1 tablespoon	minced fresh parsley	15 mL
	Salt and pepper	
1/4 cup	dry white wine	50 mL
2 tablespoons	red currant jelly	25 mL
2 teaspoons	soy sauce	10 mL
1 teaspoon	lemon juice	5 mL
1/8 teaspoon	paprika	0.5 mL

1. Sprinkle the inside of each hen with freshly ground black pepper and a dash of salt if desired.

2. Put butter and onion in a medium bowl. Microwave on High for 1 to 2 minutes or until onion is soft. Stir in rice, thyme, pecans and parsley. Season to taste with salt and pepper.

3. Spoon half of the rice mixture into each hen. Tie legs together, tuck wings under the hens and place the hens breast down on a microwave-safe platter.

4. Warm wine, jelly, soy sauce, lemon juice and paprika and pour over hens. Cover with waxed paper and microwave on High for 8 minutes.

5. Turn hens so that the breast is up; rotate hens a quarter turn (the side that faced the center of the pan for the first half of the cooking is now facing the outer edge of the pan). Brush with wine mixture. Remove waxed paper and microwave on High for 15 to 18 minutes, or until juices run clear when you pierce the breast of the hen with a sharp knife. Baste occasionally with pan juices during cooking. Let stand for 10 minutes before serving.

Makes 2 servings.

Regular Oven Method – CORNISH HENS WITH WILD RICE

Baste hens and bake in a 425° F (220° C) oven for 15 minutes. Lower heat to 350° F (180° C), add 1/2 cup (125 mL) chicken stock or apple juice to the pan and bake for 1 hour more, basting occasionally. Hens will be tender and brown when cooked.

FOR ONE SERVING

Cut stuffing quantities in half and microwave stuffing for 1 minute. Microwave one hen on High, covered with waxed paper, for 5 minutes, then uncovered for 3 to 5 minutes, or until hen tests done. Baste as indicated above. Let stand 7 minutes.

CURRIED CHICKEN SALAD WITH FRUIT

Using your microwave to cook the components for salads will keep the preparation time short and sweet. If you plan to carry this salad to the cottage or campsite, be sure to refrigerate well to prevent spoilage.

2	whole chicken breasts, halved	2
	Salt and pepper	
2	green onions, chopped	2
1 cup	peeled, seeded, diced cucumber	250 mL
1	tin mandarin oranges, drained, juice reserved	1
1/2 cup	sliced celery	125 mL
1 cup	seedless green or red grapes	250 mL
1/2 cup	mayonnaise	125 mL
2 teaspoons	curry powder, or to taste	10 mL
1/2 cup	blanched, salted peanuts	125 mL

1. Arrange chicken pieces in a circle around the edge of a microwave-safe baking dish with the thicker part of each piece facing the outer edge of the dish. Sprinkle lightly with salt and pepper. Cover with waxed paper. Microwave on High for 4 to 7 minutes per pound. The length of cooking time varies with the size and shape of the pieces. Rotate the chicken pieces in the pan every few minutes to allow even cooking. Chicken is fully cooked when the juices run clear when you pierce the thickest part of the piece with a sharp knife. Cool the chicken pieces, then remove skin and bones. Chop the meat into bitesize pieces and refrigerate until cold.

2. Toss chicken with the onion, cucumber, oranges, celery, and grapes.

3. Combine mayonnaise and curry powder in a small bowl. Mix in 4 teaspoons of the reserved juice from the oranges.

4. Stir mayonnaise mixture into the chicken mixture. Taste and season with salt, pepper and more curry if desired. Sprinkle with peanuts. Serve cold. This salad can be prepared a day ahead and refrigerated until serving time.

Makes 6 servings.

CRANBERRY STUFFED TURKEY BREAST

If you plan to serve this elegant entrée for Christmas dinner, use cranberry chutney as I have done. When I serve it the rest of the year, I use a mixed fruit or mango chutney instead.

1	turkey breast half, about 1 1/2 pounds (750 g) butterflied and flattened Salt and pepper	1
3	slices bacon, chopped	3
2	green onions, chopped	2
1	clove garlic, minced	1
1	carrot, peeled, cut into thin strips	1
1/2 cup	cranberry chutney	125 mL
3 tablespoons	pecan halves Olive oil or melted butter	50 mL

1. Sprinkle turkey breast lightly with salt and pepper. Refrigerate until needed.

2. Combine bacon, onion and garlic in a glass measuring cup and microwave on High for 4 minutes, or until bacon is cooked. Drain off bacon fat.

3. Place carrot and 1 tablespoon (15 mL) water in a microwave-safe dish. Cover tightly with plastic wrap and microwave on High for 2 minutes, or until carrot is tender. Drain.

4. To assemble: Spread chutney to cover the turkey breast. Sprinkle bacon mixture over chutney. Place carrot pieces on top in parallel lines, then sprinkle pecans over all. Roll up like a jelly roll and tie with string.

5. Rub surface of the roll lightly with olive oil or melted butter. Place on a microwave-safe plate and microwave on Medium-high for 10 minutes per pound (500 g) (calculate time using the total weight, including stuffing ingredients), or until the temperature probe or a meat thermometer registers 170° F (80° C). Let stand for 10 minutes to finish cooking and to make meat easier to slice. When you check the internal temperature after standing, time, it should be 185° F (90° C).

6. Pan drippings can be degreased and drizzled over the slices just before serving.

7. Slice, arrange on a platter and garnish with parsley sprigs.

Makes 3 to 4 servings.

MICROWAVE HINT – TEMPERATURE PROBE

If you are using a temperature probe to cook poultry, be sure that the tip of the probe is touching meat rather than stuffing (difficult to do, since you cannot see inside the roll!).

You can check this in the following way: When the oven stops, indicating that the poultry is cooked, move the probe to a new position near the center of the roast and reset microwave to 170° F (80° C). Press Start: it will stop immediately if the internal temperature has reached 170° F (80° C).

TARRAGON STUFFED CHICKEN BREASTS

If you don't have fresh tarragon, use 1 1/4 teaspoons (6 mL) dried.

4	chicken breast halves, skinned, deboned and flattened	4
	Salt and pepper	
5 tablespoons	soft butter	65 mL
4 teaspoons	minced fresh tarragon leaves (can use fresh or dried basil instead)	20 mL
2 teaspoons	minced fresh chives	10 mL
1 teaspoon	minced fresh parsley	5 mL
1/3 cup	grated Mozzarella cheese	75 mL
	Flour	
1	egg, beaten with 1 tablespoon (15 mL) water	1
2 tablespoons	dry breadcrumbs	25 mL
1/4 cup	toasted ground almonds	50 mL
1 tablespoon	Parmesan cheese	15 mL
1/2 teaspoon	paprika	2 mL
1/4 cup	dry white wine	50 mL

1. Sprinkle each chicken breast lightly with salt and pepper.

2. Combine butter, tarragon or basil, chives and parsley in a small bowl. Set aside 2 tablespoons (25 mL) of this herb butter mixture.

3. Mix remaining herb butter with grated mozzarella. Shape into 4 sticks and place 1 stick on top of each chicken piece. Roll chicken up tightly around herbed cheese stick, tucking in ends if possible, and securing each roll with a toothpick.

4. Coat rolls with flour, then dip in egg/water mixture. Combine breadcrumbs, almonds, Parmesan and paprika, and dip chicken pieces in this mixture to coat well. Rolls can be refrigerated overnight at this point.

5. Place chicken rolls in a shallow microwave-safe casserole. Melt reserved herb butter and pour over rolls. Pour wine into dish around rolls. Cover casserole with waxed paper and microwave on Medium for 10 minutes, or until chicken is no longer pink. Increase cooking time slightly if chicken has been refrigerated.

Makes 4 servings.

Regular Oven Method – TARRAGON STUFFED CHICKEN BREASTS

Place chicken rolls in pan and roast at 350° F (180° C) for 15 minutes before adding wine. Add wine and continue to cook for 35 minutes more. Spoon pan juices over the chicken breast rolls when serving.

MICROWAVE HINT

Soften butter in the microwave and combine with minced fresh garlic, grated lemon rind to taste, freshly ground pepper and your favourite minced fresh herbs. Spread on sliced French bread. Place slices in a wicker basket (make sure there are no hidden wires in the basket), cover with a paper towel or tea towel and microwave on High until butter melts and bread is hot. Time needed will vary with quantity. Or wrap buttered loaf in foil and place on warming rack of barbecue for about 20 minutes, or until hot.

Turkey Fajitas

Serve fajitas buffet-style. Put all of the ingredients out and let each guest assemble their own. Provide lots of serviettes: fajitas are messy but fun!

2 tablespoons	oil	25 mL
1	large clove garlic, minced	1
1/2 cup	chopped onion	125 mL
1	green pepper, cut into strips	1
1	red pepper, cut into strips	1
1 1/4 cups	Mexican Hot Sauce, divided (recipe on page 64)	300 mL
3 cups	cooked turkey strips	750 mL
	Guacamole (recipe on page 92)	
	Sour cream	
	Sliced black olives	
1	package of 6 or 8-inch (15 to 20 cm) flour tortillas	1

1. Place oil, garlic and onion in a large microwave-safe casserole. Microwave on High for 2 minutes. Stir in green and red peppers and microwave on High for 2 minutes or until vegetables are crisp-tender.

2. Add 1/4 cup (50 mL) Hot Sauce and turkey; toss to mix well. Taste and add more sauce if needed. Microwave on High for 1 to 2 minutes, or until mixture is heated through. Cover and keep warm.

3. Wrap several tortillas in paper towelling or a clean tea towel and warm in the microwave on High until hot (time will depend on how many are being heated – one or two tortillas take less than 30 seconds).

4. Place remaining Hot Sauce, Guacamole, sour cream and olives in small serving dishes. Spoon some of the turkey mixture onto a warm tortilla and add the toppings of your choice. Roll the tortilla around the filling.

Makes 4 to 6 servings.

CHEESE CANNELONI

If you don't want to make your own pasta for this recipe, purchase fresh pasta lasagne, then cut the strips into 5 x 3-inch (12 x 7 cm) squares.

l pound	Ricotta cheese	500 g
1/4 pound	Mozzarella cheese, shredded	125 g
1/4 cup	freshly grated Parmesan cheese	50 mL
1	egg	1
1/2 teaspoon	salt, or to taste	2 mL
1/4 teaspoon	freshly ground pepper	1 mL
1 tablespoon	minced fresh parsley	15 mL
12	squares freshly made pasta Quick Tomato Sauce (recipe on page)	12

1. In a medium bowl combine Ricotta, Mozzarella, 1 tablespoon (15 mL) Parmesan, egg, salt, pepper and parsley. Divide mixture into 12 portions and spread one portion along one edge of each pasta square. Roll up pasta squares and place them, seam side down, in a lightly greased microwave-safe baking dish large enough to hold all rolls in a single layer. Spoon Tomato Sauce over and sprinkle with remaining Parmesan.

2. Cover with microwave-safe plastic wrap (vented to allow steam to escape) and microwave on Medium for 20 to 25 minutes, or until entire casserole is hot and bubbly. Let stand, covered for 10 minutes before serving.

Makes 4 to 6 servings.

MICROWAVE HINT FOR NEW OWNERS – COVERING FOOD

How you cover food in the microwave determines the texture of the finished product. Covering tightly with microwave-safe plastic wrap will steam the food and make it very moist. Leaving a small opening at the edge of the dish will allow some steam to escape. Covering with waxed paper will hold in some moisture. Waxed paper is often used to prevent splattering during cooking. Rolls and sandwiches are often wrapped in paper towels to keep them from drying out.

When you are trying to decide whether or not to cover, do the same as you would if you were cooking that food in the conventional way.

Regular Oven Method – GREEN CORN ENCHILADAS

Prepare sauce over medium heat on the stovetop. Bake assembled dish at 425° F (220° C) for 20 to 25 minutes, or until hot and bubbly.

GREEN CORN ENCHILADAS

I was given this recipe by my very special friend and pen pal since 1958, Patti Miller of Bozeman, Montana. Patti grew up in Phoenix, Arizona, and is a Mexican food fanatic. This recipe is wonderful.

12	6-inch (15 cm) corn tortillas	12
	Oil for frying	
3/4 cup	chopped green onion	175 mL
2 cups	Monterey Jack Cheese (or brick cheese)	500 mL
2 tablespoons	butter	25 mL
2 tablespoons	flour	25 mL
1 cup	chicken stock	250 mL
1/2 cup	sour cream	125 mL
1/2	of a 4-ounce (114 mL) tin diced green chilies	1/2
	tomato salsa	
	Mexican Hot Sauce (see recipe on page 64)	
	Garnishes: sour cream, chopped fresh tomatoes and shredded lettuce	

1. Heat enough oil to cover bottom of small skillet. Fry tortillas quickly (about 10 seconds per side) and drain on paper towels.

2. Place 2 tablespoons (25 mL) grated cheese and a bit of onion on each tortilla and roll up. Place filled tortillas seam side down in a lightly greased, rectangular baking pan.

3. To make sauce: Melt butter in a 2-cup (500 mL) glass measure on High for 30 seconds. Stir in flour with a whisk. Gradually whisk in stock. Microwave on High for 2 1/2 minutes, or until thickened. Stir halfway through. Stir in sour cream and drained, diced chilies.

4. Pour sauce over tortillas and sprinkle with a bit of paprika. Cover with waxed paper and microwave on High for 9 to 11 minutes, or until and sauce is bubbly.

5. Top individual servings with Mexican Hot Sauce and desired garnishes.

Makes 6 servings.

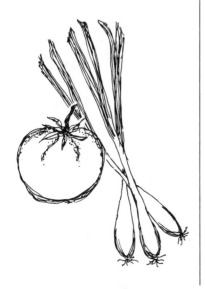

HAM LOAF

Serve this for brunch with scrambled eggs or a vegetable frittata, fresh fruit, warm breakfast pastries and good, hot coffee.

l tablespoon	butter	15 mL
1/2 cup	chopped onion	125 mL
1	clove garlic, minced	1
1 pound	lean smoked ham, finely ground	500 g
1/3 cup	minced fresh parsley	75 mL
1/2 cup	fine dry breadcrumbs	125 mL
1/2 teaspoon	dry mustard	2 mL
	Pinch of nutmeg and ground cloves	
2	eggs	2
2 tablespoons	milk	25 mL
2 teaspoons	Worcestershire sauce	10 mL
	Freshly ground pepper to taste	

1. Place butter, onion and garlic in an 8-cup (2 L) glass casserole or measuring cup. Microwave on High for 2 to 3 minutes, or until onion is soft.

2. Stir ham, parsley, breadcrumbs, mustard, nutmeg and cloves into onion mixture.

3. Mix eggs, milk, Worcestershire sauce and pepper together. Add to ham mixture, stirring to mix very well.

4. Shape ham mixture into a 7-inch (18 cm) ring in a lightly greased microwave-safe baking dish. Cover with waxed paper and microwave on High for 5 minutes. Lower power level to Medium-low and microwave 5 minutes more, or until loaf is firm and the internal temperature is 160° F (75° C).

5. Cool for l0 minutes, then transfer loaf to a serving plate. Serve garnished with parsley and cherry tomatoes.

Makes 6 servings.

Regular Oven Method – HAM LOAF

Sauté onion and garlic in butter in skillet on stovetop. Bake at 375° F (190° C) for 25 to 35 minutes, or until meat thermometers registers 160° F (75° C.)

MICROWAVE HINT – MEAT LOAF

Any type of meat loaf that is cooked in the microwave should be shaped into a ring or cooked in a ring pan. Loaf-shaped meat loaves will not cook evenly; the ends will overcook before the middle finishes cooking.

JAMBALAYA

Substitute hot smoked sausage, crawfish, beef or pork for the meat and fish below. The total weight of meat and fish combined should be between 1 and 1 1/2 pounds (500 - 750 g).

1 tablespoon	oil	15 mL
6 ounces	large shrimp, shelled and deveined	187.5 g
8 ounces	boneless chicken breast, cubed	250 g
6 ounces	smoked ham, cut into 1/2-inch (1 cm) cubes	187.5 g
2 teaspoons	Creole seasoning, or to taste (recipe on page 144)	10 mL
2/3 cup	chopped onion	150 mL
2/3 cup	chopped green pepper	150 mL
1/3 cup	chopped celery	75 mL
1 1/4 cups	chopped canned or fresh tomatoes	300 mL
1 1/2 tablespoons	tomato paste	25 mL
1 tablespoon	minced fresh parsley	15 mL
1 cup	chicken broth	250 mL
1 cup	long grain white rice	250 mL

1. Place oil, shrimp and chicken in a large microwave-safe casserole. Cover and microwave on High for 3 to 5 minutes, or until chicken and shrimp are cooked.

2. Add ham, Creole seasoning, onion, green pepper and celery. Microwave on High for 3 to 5 minutes, or until vegetables begin to get tender. Stir once.

3. Add tomatoes, paste, parsley and broth. Microwave on High for 5 to 7 minutes or until mixture comes to a boil. Stir in rice. Cover and microwave on Medium-low for 20 minutes, or until rice is cooked.

Stir to mix well and serve hot.

Makes 4 generous servings.

MICROWAVE MAKE-AHEAD MEALS

When you make your favourite casserole, double the recipe and freeze individual servings to heat in the microwave.

CREOLE SEASONING

This is a general purpose seasoning mix and can be used on grilled meat, fish or poultry. Sprinkle it on fish fillets brushed with melted butter before cooking them in the microwave for a zesty taste treat. Store extra in a tightly covered jar in the cupboard.

l tablespoon	dried basil	15 mL
l 1/2 tablespoons	paprika	25 mL
l tablespoon	dried oregano	15 mL
l 1/2 teaspoons	dried thyme	7 mL
l teaspoon	garlic powder	5 mL
1/2 teaspoon	cayenne	2 mL
1/2 teaspoon	mace	2 mL
1/4 teaspoon	black pepper	1 mL
l	bay leaf	1

Grind all ingredients in a blender or food processor until the bay leaf is very finely chopped. Store in an airtight container.

Makes about l/4 cup (50 mL).

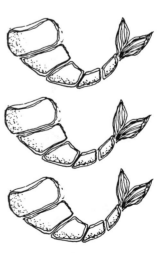

MACARONI AND CHEESE

Instead of cheddar cheese, I often use up any little end pieces of cheese I find lurking in my refrigerator. The results are often surprisingly delicious.

3 tablespoons	butter	50 mL
3 tablespoons	flour	50 mL
1/2 teaspoon	salt	2 mL
	Dash of pepper	
1 1/2 cups	milk	375 mL
1 cup	grated sharp cheddar cheese	250 mL
1 1/4 cups	macaroni, cooked and drained	300 mL

TOPPING:

2 tablespoons	crumbled corn chips, sesame seeds or breadcrumbs	25 mL

1. Place butter in an 8-cup (2 L) glass measure or bowl. Microwave on High for 30 seconds or until melted.

2. Stir in flour, salt and pepper all at once. Gradually whisk in milk until well blended. Microwave on Medium for 5 to 6 minutes, or until hot and thick. Whisk twice during cooking.

3. Add cheese and stir until melted. Stir in cooked macaroni and mix well. Taste and adjust seasonings.

4. Pour mixture into a buttered casserole and sprinkle with desired topping. Microwave on Medium for 3 minutes. If you use a probe, set it to 160° F (75° C).

Makes 4 servings.

MICROWAVE HINT – SMOOTH SAUCES

Microwave cream sauce will be smooth if you follow these simple steps:

Δ melt butter in a large glass measuring cup or bowl.
Δ add flour all at once and stir well with a whisk.
Δ whisk in milk. Microwave on Medium, whisking every two minutes, until the sauce thickens.

Homemade Pizza

If you're looking for a family cooking project that is fun and sure to please everyone, try making pizza from scratch. This dough recipe makes enough for 3 12-inch (30 cm) pizza shells, so freeze the extra dough in 2 balls, ready to defrost in the microwave.

1	tin (7 1/2 ounce [213 mL]) tomato sauce	1
	garlic sauce	
	oregano	
	freshly ground pepper	
1	recipe Pizza Dough (recipe follows)	1

Toppings: Mozzarella cheese, pepperoni, sliced fresh tomatoes, green pepper slices, sliced mushrooms, ham, bacon, anchovies, olives or your favourites.

Pizza Dough

l/2 cup	warm water	125 mL
l teaspoon	sugar	5 mL
l	package (l tablespoon [15 mL]) active dry yeast	1
6 cups	flour	1.5 L
1/2 teaspoon	salt	2 mL
1/2 cup	wheat germ or oat bran (optional)	125 mL
3 tablespoons	vegetable oil	50 mL
l l/2 cups	warm water	375 mL

1. Dissolve sugar in water in a small bowl or cup. Sprinkle in yeast and let stand l0 minutes, or until mixture is bubbly. Stir.

2. In a large bowl combine flour, salt and wheat germ or oat bran. Stir in oil, then yeast mixture. Add warm water and mix with your hands until moist but not sticky. Add more flour if too sticky. Knead on a lightly floured surface for 5 minutes, or until smooth. (Kneading is easier if you wash the dough bits from your hands before you begin to knead.)

3. To proof dough in the microwave: Place dough in a large, well-greased microwave-safe bowl. Brush the top with oil, then cover bowl with plastic wrap.

4. Put 3 cups (750 mL) water in a square baking dish, then set the bowl of dough in this dish. Microwave on Warm for 25 to 30 minutes, or until dough doubles in bulk.

5. Punch dough down. Divide into smaller balls, and freeze some of the dough, if desired.

Makes enough dough for 3 12-inch (30 cm) pizzas, or several smaller ones.

TO ASSEMBLE YOUR PIZZA

1. Spread dough to desired thickness on a baking sheet or pizza pan. Spread with tomato sauce and sprinkle with garlic salt, oregano and freshly ground pepper to taste.

2. Add your favourite toppings.

For an interesting change try one of these topping combinations:

Δ Sliced tomatoes, pesto sauce, mozzarella, fontina cheese
Δ Grilled eggplant, sautéed onions, sun dried tomatoes, mozzarella, provolone, garlic
Δ Sliced tomatoes, capers, red onions, olives, hot chilies, mozzarella, fontina cheese
Δ Marinated leeks, feta cheese, roasted red peppers, garlic, mozzarella

3. Once you have assembled your pizza or individual pizzas, bake in a preheated 450° F (230° C) oven for 15 minutes, or until cheese is bubbly.

COOKING TIP – FOCACCIA

For an interesting Italian appetizer called Focaccia, prick a thin pizza crust all over with a fork. Spread with shallots and garlic sautéed in olive oil, then sprinkle with fresh herbs, salt and pepper, and Parmesan cheese, if desired. Bake in a 400° F (200° C) oven for 15 to 20 minutes or until slightly brown and crisp.

JUGGED HARE

Rabbit is low in fat and cholesterol, high in protein and is easily digested because it contains a low amount of fibrous connective tissue. I have used domestic rabbit rather than hare in this recipe, though either is acceptable.

1	rabbit or hare, cut into serving pieces	1
	Freshly ground pepper	
2	small onions, each stuck with 2 whole cloves	2
1	clove garlic, minced	1
1/2	lemon, thinly sliced	1/2
	Few sprigs of parsley	
1/4 teaspoon	dried rosemary or thyme leaves (1 teaspoon [5 mL] fresh)	1 mL
1/2 cup	dry white wine	125 mL
2 to 3 cups	boiling beef or chicken stock	500 to 750 mL
	Paprika	
1 1/2 tablespoons	cornstarch	25 mL
3 tablespoons	dry white wine (second amount)	50 mL
1 tablespoon	cold water	15 mL

1. Sprinkle rabbit pieces lightly with pepper. In a large microwave-safe casserole or simmer pot, layer rabbit pieces with onions, garlic, lemon, parsley, and rosemary or thyme. Pour in wine.

2. Heat stock to boiling, then pour into casserole until all rabbit pieces are covered with liquid. Use a heatproof plate or simmer pot insert to keep the pieces submerged in the liquid. Microwave on High for 8 minutes, or until liquid boils. Lower power to Medium-low and microwave for 30 to 45 minutes, or until meat is tender.

3. Transfer meat to a heated platter, sprinkle with paprika and keep warm.

4. Combine cornstarch, 3 tablespoons (50 mL) wine and water in a 4-cup (1 L) glass measure. Add 1 cup (250 mL) rabbit cooking liquid (discard vegetables). Microwave on High for 4 minutes, stirring occasionally, until liquid thickens. Taste and add salt and pepper as needed.

5. Spoon some sauce over meat and pass the rest.

Makes 4 servings.

Rosemary

MICROWAVE HINT – COOKING RABBIT

Because rabbit meat is so lean, it benefits from slow, moist cooking. Even in the microwave, simmering slowly produces best results.

RABBIT BOURGUIGNON

This recipe is adapted from a brochure of rabbit recipes put out by the Ontario Ministry of Agriculture and Food.

1	rabbit, front and back legs only	1
3/4 cup	dry red wine	175 mL
1	bay leaf	1
8	peppercorns	8
2	slices bacon, chopped	2
2 cups	sliced mushrooms	500 mL
1	medium onion, chopped	1
1	carrot, thinly sliced	1
1	clove garlic, minced	1
1 cup	chicken stock	250 mL
1/4 cup	minced fresh parsley	50 mL
1 teaspoon	dried thyme	5 mL
1 tablespoon	soft butter	15 mL
2 tablespoons	flour	25 mL

1. Place rabbit pieces, wine, bay leaf and peppercorns in a glass casserole dish. Cover and refrigerate 3 hours or overnight, turning pieces occasionally.

2. Place bacon in a large casserole and microwave on High for 2 minutes. Stir in mushrooms, onion, carrot and garlic and microwave on High for 6 minutes or until carrots are tender.

3. Stir in stock, parsley and thyme, then add rabbit pieces and marinade. Remove peppercorns. Make sure that rabbit pieces are completely submerged in the liquid. Add more stock if necessary.

4. Cover casserole tightly and microwave on High for 5 minutes, or until liquid comes to a boil. Microwave on Medium-low for 30 to 45 minutes, or until meat is tender.

5. Lift rabbit pieces from sauce using a slotted spoon. Remove bay leaf.

6. Combine butter and flour together until smooth. Stir butter mixture into the hot sauce. Microwave on High for 2 minutes or until sauce thickens and no raw flour taste remains. Stir occasionally. Taste and season with pepper and salt. Return rabbit pieces to the thickened sauce. Serve over hot cooked pasta.

Makes 4 servings.

MICROWAVE HINT

Rearranging serving-size pieces of meat during microwave cooking will help the pieces cook more evenly. If your microwave oven does not have a turntable, rotate the dish as well.

Meatless Italian Lasagne

This is a microwave adaptation of the recipe that won second prize in the Zucchini category of the 1990 *Ottawa Citizen* recipe contest, but it was my favourite. Use no-cook lasagne noodles when you prepare it, and make it in two 8-inch (22 cm) baking pans instead of a 13 x 9-inch (34 x 22 cm) pan, if you wish. Freeze the second one for another day.

1/4 cup	margarine or butter	50 mL
2	medium carrots, finely chopped	2
2	stalks celery, finely chopped	2
1	medium green pepper, chopped	1
2	medium onions, chopped	2
2	medium zucchini, sliced	2
1	19-ounce (540 mL) tin tomatoes, cut up	1
1 cup	water	250 mL
1	12-ounce (341 mL) tin tomato paste	1
2	bay leaves	2
2 or 3	cloves garlic, minced	2 or 3
1/4 cup	snipped parsley	50 mL
1 teaspoon	dried basil, crushed	5 mL
3/4 teaspoon	salt	3 mL
1/2 teaspoon	dried oregano, crushed	2 mL
1/2 teaspoon	dried thyme, crushed	2 mL
1/4 teaspoon	pepper	1 mL
2 cups	sliced fresh mushrooms (optional)	500 mL
10	no-cook lasagne noodles	10
2 cups	cream-style cottage cheese	500 mL
8 ounces	Mozzarella cheese, shredded	250 g
1/4 cup	grated Parmesan cheese	50 mL

1. In a large microwave-safe casserole, melt butter. Stir in carrots, celery, green pepper and onion. Microwave on High for 8 to 10 minutes, or until vegetables are tender. Stir once.

2. Add zucchini, tomatoes and juice, water, tomato paste, bay leaves, garlic, parsley and seasonings and mix well. Microwave on High for 20 minutes, stirring often, until

mixture has thickened. Stir in mushrooms if desired. Microwave on High for 5 minutes more. Remove and discard bay leaves.

3. Use 2 8-inch ((20 cm) round or 1 rectangular 13 x 9-inch (34 x 22 cm) microwave-safe baking pan. Layer the ingredients in the following order for each of 2 pans:

- 1 cup(250 mL) sauce (2 cups [500 mL] for rectangular pan)
- a layer of noodles
- 1 cup (250 mL) sauce (2 cups [500 mL] for rectangular pan)
- half of the cottage cheese (all of the cheese for rectangular pan)
- half of the mozzarella (all of the cheese for rectangular pan)
- layer of noodles
- half of remaining sauce (all remaining sauce for rectangular pan)

Cover pans with microwave-safe plastic wrap.

4. **For 2 round pans**: Microwave each pan on High for 10 minutes, then on Medium-low for 15 to 20 minutes or until noodles are tender. **For rectangular pan**: Microwave on High for 15 minutes, then on Medium-low for 20 to 25 minutes, or until noodles are tender. If lasagne seems to be cooking unevenly, rotate the dish partway through cooking.

5. Remove plastic wrap and sprinkle lasagne with Parmesan cheese. Microwave on High for 1 minute, or until cheese melts. Let stand, covered, for 10 minutes before serving.

Makes 8 servings.

MICROWAVE HINT – CHEESE TOPPINGS

Add cheese toppings to casseroles near the end of the cooking time. Cheese, especially Mozzarella, toughens if cooking continues after cheese has melted.

NAVARIN PRINTEMPS

This light and delicious lamb and vegetable stew suits
April dinner parties beautifully. Serve it with tiny new
potatoes, steamed asparagus or broccoli, and a crisp salad.

3 pounds	lean lamb	1.5 kg
1/2 teaspoon	salt	2 mL
1 teaspoon	sugar	5 mL
1/2 teaspoon	pepper	2 mL
1/4 teaspoon	nutmeg	1 mL
2 tablespoons	vegetable oil	25 mL
1 cup	chopped onion	250 mL
1	clove garlic, minced	1
3 tablespoons	flour	50 mL
3 cups	beef or lamb stock	750 mL
1 tablespoon	fresh rosemary leaves	15 mL
	(or 1 teaspoon [5 mL] dried)	
1 tablespoon	tomato paste	15 mL
1 cup	diced carrot	250 mL
1 cup	diced turnip	250 mL
1 cup	diced potato (omit if	250 mL
	you plan to serve new	
	potatoes, rice or pasta	
	with the stew)	

1. Trim visible fat from lamb and cut lamb into 1-inch (2.5
cm) cubes.

2. Combine salt, sugar, pepper and nutmeg and sprinkle
over lamb cubes.

3. Heat oil in a large skillet and brown lamb cubes and
onion together on the stovetop over medium-high heat. A
large, deep browning dish can be used for this step if
desired. Remove accumulated liquid from the pan.

4. Stir in garlic and flour. Gradually add half of the stock,
stirring to mix brown bits on the bottom of the pan into the
sauce.

5. Transfer lamb mixture to a large microwave-safe
casserole. Add remaining ingredients and stir to mix well.
Submerge a heatproof plate or simmer pot insert in the

stew to keep meat and vegetable pieces from floating on the surface. (Pieces allowed to float on the top will become overcooked and very tough).

6. Cover pan and microwave on High for 10 minutes, or until the mixture is almost boiling. Microwave on Low for 45 minutes to 1 hour, or until meat and vegetable pieces are tender.

7. Refrigerate overnight, then skim off fat. Reheat stew until hot. If you wish to have a thick gravy, stir in 2 tablespoons (25 mL) cornstarch dissolved in 1/4 cup (50 mL) cold water. Microwave on High for 5 minutes, stirring occasionally, until thickened. Taste and adjust seasonings. Sprinkle each serving with finely minced fresh parsley.

Makes 4 to 6 servings.

MICROWAVE HINT – TENDER STEW MEAT AND VEGETABLES

Producing a microwave stew in which all meat and vegetable pieces are tender and moist is not a difficult task. Cooking time must be long enough to soften vegetables such as carrots, or this type of hard vegetable should be precooked. For tender meat, cook the stew a day before you plan to serve it; refrigerate overnight. This "mellowing" time will produce melt-in-your-mouth results. Skim off any fat before reheating.

Ratatouille

Made in the summer with field-ripened tomatoes, eggplant and zucchini, this Mediterranean dish is at its best. When I make it in the winter, I add a tin of tomato paste to make up for the pale colour and flavour of winter tomatoes.

l tablespoon	oil	15 mL
l cup	chopped onion	250 mL
3	cloves garlic, minced	3
1	medium eggplant, peeled, diced (3 cups [750 mL] diced)	1
1 1/2 cups	diced zucchini	375 mL
1	large sweet red or green pepper, chopped	1
2 cups	chopped tomatoes	500 mL
l tablespoon	minced fresh basil leaves (1 teaspoon [5 mL] dried)	15 mL
2 tablespoons	vinegar	25 mL
	Salt, pepper and Tabasco or minced jalapeno peppers to taste	

1. Place oil, onion and garlic in a large microwave-safe casserole. Stir to coat vegetables with oil. Microwave on High for 3 to 4 minutes, or until onion is soft.

2. Add eggplant, zucchini, peppers, tomatoes, basil and vinegar and microwave on High for 15 to 20 minutes, or until vegetables are soft and slightly thickened. Stir every 5 minutes during cooking.

3. Add salt, pepper and Tabasco or jalapenos to taste. Cover and refrigerate until cold. (This chilling helps to blend flavors.)

4. Serve hot, cold, or at room temperature.

Makes 4 to 6 servings.

Microwave Hint – Corn on the Cob

Melt butter in a small microwaveable serving dish and pass with a small brush to butter corn on the cob.

SAUSAGE STUFFING WITH FRUIT AND NUTS

This delicious mixture stuffs every holiday bird roasted in our house. I make the stuffing several weeks ahead and freeze it, then defrost it and stuff the turkey or homegrown chicken just before roasting.

1 pound	bulk sausage meat, defrosted	500 g
1 cup	chopped celery	250 mL
1 cup	chopped onion	250 mL
1 teaspoon	crumbled dried sage leaves, or to taste	5 mL
1/2 teaspoon	pepper	2 mL
1	apple,peeled, cored and chopped	1
1/3 cup	chopped dried apricots or raisins	75 mL
1/2 cup	coarsely chopped hazelnuts, pecans or pistachios	125 mL
1 to 2 cups	dried breadcrumbs	250 to 500 mL
	Salt to taste	

1. Crumble sausage meat into a large microwave-safe casserole. Microwave on High for 3 minutes.

2. Add celery and onion and stir. Microwave on High for 5 to 6 minutes, or until sausage is cooked and vegetables are soft. Stir once during cooking.

3. Stir in sage, pepper,apple, apricots and nuts. Add enough breadcrumbs to absorb excess moisture in the mixture. The stuffing should still have a moist texture. Taste and adjust seasonings. Cover and refrigerate or freeze until cooking time. Do not stuff the bird ahead of time.

Makes about 8 cups (2 L) of stuffing, enough for an 8 to 10 pound (4 or 5 kg) turkey or chicken.

MICROWAVE HINT – PLUMP RAISINS

Before adding to stuffing, cakes or muffins, pour water, juice or sherry over raisins in a small microwave-safe dish and microwave on High for 1 to 2 minutes, or until hot. Let stand for 10 minutes before using.

Spanakopita (Greek Spinach Pie)

This dish has a crust of phyllo pastry, one of the foods that cannot be successfully cooked in the microwave. By making the filling in the microwave, however, you greatly reduce the preparation time.

1/2 cup	salt	125 mL
1 1/4 pounds	fresh spinach, washed, stems removed	625 g
1 cup	chopped onion	250 mL
2 tablespoons	oil	25 mL
4	eggs	4
1 cup	ricotta cheese	250 mL
1 cup	crumbled feta cheese	250 mL
1/2 cup	firmly packed fresh dill	125 mL
	Salt and freshly ground pepper to taste	
2/3 cup	melted butter	150 mL
6 to 8	sheets phyllo, defrosted	6 to 8

1. Place salt and spinach in a large bowl or sinkful of cold water and let stand for 30 minutes. Drain spinach and rinse well with cold water.

2. Place onion and oil in a large microwave-safe casserole. Microwave on High for 4 minutes, or until onion is soft. Stir once.

3. Add spinach. Cover tightly and microwave on High for 7 to 9 minutes or until spinach wilts. Stir spinach twice during cooking. Drain spinach mixture in a colander in the sink or over a bowl. Chop coarsely – scissors work well for this.

4. Beat eggs and ricotta in a large bowl until smooth. Stir in feta cheese, dill and spinach mixture. Add salt and pepper to taste.

5. To assemble: Butter a 13 x 9-inch (34 x 22 cm) baking pan and place 1 layer of phyllo in the pan (about 1/2 of a sheet). Brush with melted butter. Repeat with 5 more layers, brushing each layer lightly with butter. Spoon filling into the pan in an even layer. Top with 6 more layers of buttered phyllo.

6. Bake at 350° F (180° C) for 45 minutes, or until brown and crisp. Spanakopita can be frozen. Cool before freezing.

Makes 6 to 8 servings.

Microwave Hint – Phyllo Pastry

Whenever you see a list of foods that you cannot cook in the microwave, phyllo pastry is always mentioned. Phyllo requires a hot, dry oven to produce the crisp, flaky texture that makes it so enjoyable. Phyllo cooked or reheated in the microwave is soggy and tough. Foods made with phyllo can be defrosted in the microwave. Time needed depends on quantity being defrosted. For a very large amount, use Low power rather than Defrost. Once food is defrosted and slightly warm, place in a 400° F (200° C) oven for 5 minutes, or until pastry is crisp.

The Best of
SWEETS
&
TREATS

APPLE OATMEAL SQUARES

These squares are terrific for packed lunches. They taste just like apple crisp, but they're finger food.

1 cup	flour	250 mL
3/4 cup	lightly packed brown sugar	175 mL
1/2 teaspoon	baking soda	2 mL
1 cup	rolled oats	250 mL
1/4 cup	butter or margarine, melted	50 mL
3 tablespoons	milk	50 mL
1/2 teaspoon	cinnamon	2 mL
1/3 cup	brown sugar (second amount)	75 mL
2 teaspoons	flour (second amount)	10 mL
2 1/2 cups	peeled, sliced apples	625 mL

1. Combine flour 3/4 cup (175 mL) brown sugar, baking soda and oats in a large bowl. Add melted butter and milk and stir until well mixed and crumbly. Press half of this mixture firmly into a lightly greased 8-inch (20 cm) round or square glass baking dish. Microwave on Medium for 5 minutes.

2. Combine cinnamon, 1/3 cup (75 mL) brown sugar, and 2 teaspoons (10 mL) flour in a small bowl and stir to mix. Toss with apple slices. Spoon this mixture onto the oatmeal base.

3. Sprinkle remaining oatmeal mixture evenly over the apples and press lightly onto apples. Microwave on High for 5 to 7 minutes, or until apples are tender. Cool completely before cutting.

Makes 16 squares.

Regular Oven Method – APPLE OATMEAL SQUARES

Bake assembled dish at 350° F (180° C) for 30 to 35 minutes, or until apples are tender. If glass pan is used, lower oven temperature to 325° F (160° C).

BUDGET-WISE MICROWAVE GIFTS

Plastic microwave whisks, microwave egg poacher (can also be used for melting or heating small quantities of food), custard cups, glass measuring cups of all sizes, microwave-safe colander (perfect for cooking ground beef: fat drains off during cooking)

QUICK MICROWAVE DESSERT – BAKED APPLE

Wash and core 1 apple. Fill center with brown sugar, nuts or raisins if desired. Place in a small dish and microwave on High, covered, for 2 to 3 minutes, or until apple is tender. Let stand 3 minutes.

APPLESAUCE

Delicious warm or cold, or as the main ingredient in cakes or muffins. Use the type of apple that gives you the flavour you like best, either tart or sweet.

4	apples, peeled, cored and quartered	4
2 tablespoons	water	25 mL
1/4 cup	sugar, or to taste	50 mL
1/4 teaspoon	cinnamon, or to taste	1 mL

1. Place apple pieces and water in a 6-cup (1.5 L) casserole. Cover with casserole lid or plastic wrap, leaving a small opening to let steam escape. Microwave on High for 6 to 8 minutes, or until apples are soft but not mushy.

2. Mash apples with a fork, then add sugar and cinnamon. Stir well.

3. Cool in the refrigerator before serving, or serve warm if desired.

Makes 3 to 4 servings.

BRANDIED FUDGE SAUCE

Choose good quality chocolate for this sauce. Makes a welcome gift for your choco-holic friends.

6 ounces	semi-sweet chocolate	187.5 g
1/4 cup	butter	50 mL
1 cup	sifted icing sugar	250 mL
	Dash of salt	
1/2 cup	light corn syrup	125 mL
1/4 cup	hot water	50 mL
1/4 cup	brandy	50 mL
1 teaspoon	vanilla	5 mL

1. Place chocolate and butter in a large glass measuring cup or bowl. Microwave on Low for 4 to 6 minutes, or until melted. Stir every 2 minutes.

2. Stir in remaining ingredients. Pour into hot, sterilized jars, seal and refrigerate. Reheat in the jar in the microwave using Low power. Stir every minute. Heating time will vary with the amount of sauce being heated.

Makes 2 cups (500 mL).

BREAD PUDDING WITH WHISKEY SAUCE

The grown-up flavour of this fabulous dessert bears no resemblance to the Bread Pudding you remember from your childhood!

4 cups	day-old French bread, cut in 1/2-inch (1 cm) cubes	1 L
1/3 cup	dark raisins	75 mL
3/4 cup	pecan halves	175 mL
6 tablespoons	sugar	100 mL
1 1/2 teaspoons	butter	7 mL
1/2 teaspoon	cinnamon	2 mL
	Dash freshly ground nutmeg	
2 cups	light cream or homogenized milk	500 mL
2	eggs, lightly beaten	2

1. Butter an 8-inch (20 cm) round glass baking dish. Layer the bread cubes, raisins and pecans in the dish.

2. Place sugar, butter, spices and cream in a 4-cup (1 L) glass measure. Stir to mix well. Microwave on Medium for 3 to 4 minutes, or until butter melts and cream is warm.

3. Quickly whisk in eggs, then pour the cream mixture over the bread mixture in the pan. Sprinkle with a bit more cinnamon.

4. Cover with microwave-safe plastic wrap and microwave on Medium for 10 minutes, then uncovered for 1 to 2 minutes more, or until pudding is set almost to the center. Let stand 5 minutes.

5. Serve warm with Whiskey Sauce (recipe on page 161), whipped cream or ice cream. If a brown top is desired, put the pudding under the broiler for a minute or two until desired colour is achieved.

Makes 4 servings.

WHISKEY SAUCE

This sauce is best made in a double boiler, as constant stirring is needed to produce a smooth sauce.

6 tablespoons	butter	100 mL
1/2 cup	sugar	125 mL
1	egg	1
1/4 cup	bourbon whiskey	50 mL

1. Melt butter in a double boiler over hot, not boiling water.

2. Whisk eggs and sugar together in a small bowl. Slowly whisk egg mixture into the melted butter. Cook and stir until sauce thickens slightly.

3. Remove from heat and stir in bourbon. Serve at once; the sauce separates as it cools.

Makes about 3/4 cup (175 mL) sauce.

CARAMEL FLANS

Cooking individual custards such as these in the microwave saves you the hassle of baking them in a larger pan of water in the oven.

1/2 cup	sugar	125 mL
3 tablespoons	water	50 mL
2 cups	milk	500 mL
4	eggs	4
1/4 cup	sugar	50 mL
1/2 teaspoon	vanilla	2 mL
	Freshly grated nutmeg	

1. Butter 6 individual custard cups and set aside.

2. Place 1/2 cup (125 mL) sugar and the water in a 1-cup (250 mL) glass measure. Stir until well mixed. Microwave on High for 4 to 5 minutes, or until sugar mixture begins to brown lightly. Quickly pour some of the mixture into each of the prepared custard cups and tilt the cups to coat the bottom and part of the sides with the sugar mixture.

3. Place milk in a 4-cup (1 L) glass measure and microwave on Medium for 4 to 5 minutes, or until milk is scalded. (or use a temperature probe; set probe to 150° F (70° C) and use Medium power.)

4. Beat eggs, 1/4 cup (50 mL) sugar and vanilla in a small bowl. Stir a small amount of hot milk into the egg mixture to warm it up, then pour the egg mixture into the remaining milk and stir to mix well.

5. Pour milk mixture into the prepared custard cups and sprinkle with nutmeg.

6. Arrange cups in a circle on a tray. Microwave on Medium-low for 7 1/2 to 9 minutes or until custard is set. Rotate cups halfway through cooking if necessary.

7. Cool slightly, then refrigerate until cold.

8. To serve, loosen top edge of each flan with a sharp knife. Invert flans into small dessert dishes.

Makes 6 servings.

Regular Oven Method - CARAMEL FLANS

Prepare flans as above, making the caramel mixture and scalding the milk in saucepans on the stove. Place filled cups in a baking dish with 1 inch (2.5 cm) of boiling water in it. Bake at 350° F (180° C) for about 45 minutes, or until set. Cool, chill and unmould as above.

CARAMEL NUT SUNDAE SAUCE

Spoon this luscious sauce into a small decorative jar for a unique and much appreciated hostess gift.

2 tablespoons	butter	25 mL
1/2 cup	firmly packed brown sugar	125 mL
1/4 cup	light cream or milk	50 mL
2 tablespoons	chopped walnuts or pecans	25 mL
1/2 teaspoon	vanilla	2 mL

1. Place butter in a 2-cup (500 mL) glass measure. Microwave on High for 30 seconds or until melted.

2. Stir in sugar. Stir in cream or milk very slowly. Microwave on Medium for 1 minute, stirring after 30 seconds.

3. Stir in nuts and vanilla. Serve warm over vanilla or coffee ice cream. Store in the refrigerator.

Makes about 2/3 cup (150 mL).

MICROWAVE HINT – CRYSTALLIZED HONEY

Liquid honey which has crystallized can easily be liquified in the microwave. It only takes a few seconds using High power. Time needed varies with amount. Be sure to transfer the honey to a heatproof, microwave-safe container before heating. A plastic dish is not acceptable.

CARROT CAKE WITH CREAM CHEESE FROSTING

This cake tastes even better the second day, if it lasts that long!

CAKE:

1 1/4 cups	flour	300 mL
1 teaspoon	baking powder	5 mL
1 teaspoon	baking soda	5 mL
1/2 teaspoon	salt	2 mL
1 teaspoon	cinnamon	5 mL
1 cup	sugar	250 mL
3/4 cup	oil	175 mL
2	eggs	2
1 cup	grated carrots	250 mL
1	8-ounce (227 mL) tin crushed pineapple, drained	1
1/3 cup	chopped walnuts	75 mL
1 cup	grated coconut	250 mL

1. In a large bowl, mix together the flour, baking powder, baking soda, salt and cinnamon.

2. In another bowl combine the sugar, oil, eggs, carrots, pineapple, walnuts and coconut. Add to the flour mixture and stir well.

3. Line the bottom of a 9-inch (20 - 22 cm) round glass baking pan with waxed paper and invert a small greased heatproof bowl in the center (or use a greased microwave ring mould). Pour the batter into the pan. Microwave on Medium for 10 to 11 1/2 minutes, or until cake tests done with a toothpick. Let stand for 10 minutes.

4. Unmould onto a serving plate. Cool before frosting.

FROSTING:

1/4 cup	butter	50 mL
1/2 teaspoon	vanilla	2 mL
4 ounces	cream cheese	125 g
2 cups	icing sugar	500 mL

1. Using an electric mixer or food processor, mix together the butter, vanilla and cream cheese until smooth.

2. Add sugar and process until smooth. Spread on cooled cake.

Makes 8 to 10 servings.

Regular Oven Method – CARROT CAKE WITH CREAM CHEESE FROSTING

Reduce flour to 1 cup (250° mL). Bake at 350° F (180° C) for 35 to 45 minutes, or until cake tests done with a toothpick.

MICROWAVE HINT – CAKE SUCCESS IN THE MICROWAVE

Since microwave cakes often stick to the bottom of the pan, line pan with waxed paper before pouring in batter. Cakes bake more evenly in a ring pan than in a traditional baking pan.

OTHER WAYS TO "COOK" WITH HALLOWEEN TREATS

Δ Sprinkle raisins or chopped chocolate on pancakes as they cook.
Δ Use chopped treats as a garnish for yogurt or pudding.
Δ Spread crackers or bread with peanut butter or cream cheese, then make funny faces or designs with treats.
Δ Make a healthy dip to serve with potato chips. Serve some celery sticks to dip along with the chips.
Δ Heat popcorn briefly in the microwave, then sprinkle with grated cheese and chili powder or garlic salt.
Δ Sprinkle raisins on oatmeal or other breakfast cereal.
Δ Peanuts and other nutty treats can be added to coleslaw or fruit salad.
Δ Use treats in composed salads (pretzels for cat whiskers, raisins for eyes, cheezies for hair or spider legs, etc.). Complete the picture with fruit and vegetable pieces.
Δ Melt solid milk chocolate bars in the microwave using Medium power and serve with dipping fruits for instant "fondue."

CEREAL SQUARES

Make these squares with your children, using the candies they bring home on Halloween. You'll be adding some food value to the sugary treats, and having fun in the kitchen at the same time.

1/4 cup	margarine or butter	50 mL
40	large marshmallows	40
5 cups	mixed dry cereals (your choice)	1.25 L
1/2 to 1 cup	Halloween treats (peanuts, raisins, shelled sunflower seeds, chopped chocolate bars or red licorice, smarties, etc.)	125 to 250 mL

1. Lightly grease a 9-inch (22 cm) square baking pan and set aside.

2. Place margarine and marshmallows in a large microwave-safe bowl. Microwave on High for 2 to 3 minutes, stirring every minute, until marshmallows are melted.

3. Stir in remaining ingredients. Pour into prepared pan and press down firmly using a wet rubber spatula or your clean, wet hands. The water keeps the marshmallow mixture from sticking to the spatula or your hands.

4. Cut into squares when cool and firm.

Makes 25 squares.

CHARLOTTE RUSSE WITH RASPBERRY COULIS

Both parts of this elegant dessert can be made a day ahead, making it easy on the hostess on the day of the party. If you don't have a charlotte mould, use a 6-cup (1.5 L) soufflé dish.

16 to 20	soft ladyfingers, 3 inches (7.5 cm) long	16 to 20
1 cup	milk	250 mL
4	egg yolks	4
1/2 cup	sugar	125 mL
1/2 teaspoon	vanilla extract	2 mL
2 teaspoons	unflavoured gelatin	10 mL
1/4 cup	cold water	50 mL
1/2 cup	sour cream	125 mL
1/2 cup	whipping cream	125 mL
	Raspberry Coulis (recipe follows)	
	Fresh raspberries and mint leaves	

1. Use a serrated knife to split ladyfingers lengthwise into 2 flat halves each. Trim one end of several of the ladyfingers to taper to a point. Arrange trimmed ladyfingers in the bottom of a 4 or 6-cup (1 to 1.5 L) charlotte mould or round, deep casserole or soufflé dish with the pointed ends in the center, forming a sunburst pattern. The cut surfaces of the ladyfinger pieces should be facing up. (You will be unmoulding this dessert, so the bottom will become the top; for this reason, make the design as attractive as possible.) Try not to leave any spaces. Trim one end of the remaining ladyfinger halves flat, then stand them close together around the edge of the mould with the cut surface facing the center. Set aside.

2. Pour milk into a 4-cup (1 L) microwave-safe casserole and microwave on Medium until scalded but not boiling. If you use a temperature probe, set it to 150° F (70° C).

3. Whisk egg yolks and sugar together in a small bowl until thick and light yellow. Gradually whisk in hot milk until smoothly blended. Microwave on Medium, whisking every minute for 4 minutes, or until custard is smooth and

thickened slightly. Do not overheat or custard will curdle. Stir in vanilla.

4. Add gelatin to cold water in a small bowl and let stand for 5 minutes. Add gelatin mixture to hot custard and stir until gelatin melts.

5. Whip sour cream and whipping cream together until stiff. Refrigerate until needed.

6. To chill custard, half-fill a larger bowl with ice cubes and water, then set the bowl of custard in the ice water. Stir continuously until mixture is as thick as unbeaten egg white, then fold this mixture with the whipped cream mixture.

7. Spoon custard mixture into prepared mould, cover with plastic wrap and refrigerate overnight, or until firm.

8. Before unmoulding, trim off the tops of any ladyfingers above the surface level of the filling. Invert and unmould carefully onto a serving platter. Garnish the top with whole berries.

9. To serve: spoon some Raspberry Coulis onto each serving plate and place a slice of Charlotte Russe on the coulis. Garnish with a raspberry and a mint leaf, if desired.

Makes 6 to 8 servings.

MICROWAVE HINT – GELATIN MIXTURES

Some recipes, like Charlotte Russe With Raspberry Coulis, tell you to chill a gelatin mixture until slightly thickened. If you chill for too long and the mixture becomes too thick to fold, microwave on Medium to warm it up and melt it, then repeat the chilling procedure. This will not harm the finished recipe.

RASPBERRY COULIS

2	10-ounce (284 mL) packages frozen raspberries, defrosted	2
2 tablespoons	Kirsch	25 mL
	Sugar to taste	

1. Press defrosted berries (with or without juice) through a sieve. Add Kirsch, then sweeten to taste. Refrigerate until serving time.

Makes 1 cup (250 mL)

CHOCOLATE BANANA CREAM PIE

You can use a graham wafer or chocolate crumb crust for this pie, if you wish. The pie will taste somewhat sweeter.

l cup	sugar	250 mL
3 tablespoons	cornstarch	50 mL
1/4 teaspoon	salt	1 mL
2 cups	milk	500 mL
2	l-ounce (28.5 g) squares unsweetened chocolate	2
2	eggs, lightly beaten	2
l tablespoon	butter	15 mL
l teaspoon	vanilla	5 mL
2	large, ripe bananas, sliced	2
1	9-inch (22 cm) baked pie shell	1
l cup	whipping cream, whipped and sweetened to taste	250 mL
	Chocolate shavings or cocoa	

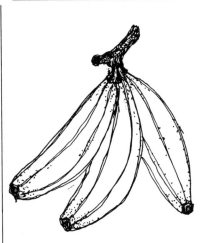

1. Place sugar, cornstach and salt in a large glass bowl or measuring cup. Whisk in milk and add chocolate. Microwave on Medium for 9 to l0 minutes, whisking occasionally, until the mixture thickens and chocolate melts.

2. Beat eggs in a small bowl. Whisk some of the hot chocolate mixture into the eggs to warm them. Slowly whisk the warm egg mixture back into the remaining chocolate mixture. Microwave on Medium for 2 minutes, stirring once, until the mixture is thick and bubbly. Add butter and vanilla and stir until butter melts.

3. Arrange sliced bananas in cooled pie shell. Pour filling over bananas to cover them completely. Refrigerate until cold.

4. Spread whipped cream over cooled filling. Garnish with chocolate shavings or a light dusting of cocoa. Refrigerate until serving time.

Makes 6 servings.

MICROWAVE HINT – OVERRIPE BANANAS

When bananas are too ripe to eat, freeze them. Defrost in the microwave, then mash and use in your favourite banana cake or muffin recipe.

Chocolate Butter Crunch

Give this as a hostess or Christmas gift in a decorative tin, or arrange on a special plate, making the container part of the gift.

1/2 cup	chopped blanched almonds	125 mL
1/2 cup	butter	125 mL
1/4 cup	ground almonds	50 mL
3/4 cup	sugar	175 mL
1 1/2 tablespoons	water	25 mL
1 1/2 teaspoons	corn syrup	7 mL
5 ounces	bittersweet or semi-sweet chocolate	150 g

1. Butter a baking sheet or jelly roll pan and set aside.

2. Place chopped almonds and 1 teaspoon (5 mL) butter in a 2-cup (500 mL) glass measure. Microwave on High for 1 minute, or until butter melts. Stir to coat almonds with butter. Microwave on High for 2 1/2 to 3 minutes, or until almonds are brown. Stir twice during cooking. Set aside.

3. Microwave the ground almonds in a small microwave-safe bowl on High for 3 minutes, or until brown. Set aside.

4. Combine remaining butter, sugar, water and corn syrup in a 4-cup (1 L) glass measure. Microwave on High, stirring occasionally, for 6 to 7 minutes, or until mixture reaches the hard crack stage (300° F, 150° C on a candy thermometer). Mixture must be removed from the microwave before using thermometer, unless it is microwave-safe. Be careful not to burn the toffee – once it reaches 200° F (100° C) it heats very quickly, so check it every few seconds.

5. Once the correct temperature is reached, quickly stir in the almond-butter mixture, then spread quickly on the buttered baking sheet. When cool and firm, invert toffee onto waxed paper.

6. Melt chocolate in microwave on Medium, checking often, for 2 to 4 minutes, or until melted. Spread one side of cooled toffee with half of the chocolate and sprinkle with half of the ground almonds. Cover with waxed paper, then carefully turn over.

7. Spread remaining chocolate on other side of toffee and sprinkle with remaining ground almonds. Chill until firm, then break into pieces.

Makes about 1 1/4 pounds (625 g).

Microwave Gift Idea

An 8 or 10-cup (2 or 2.5 L) glass measuring cup makes an excellent gift for a new microwave owner. Tie a microwave-safe whisk and spoon to the handle with a ribbon.

CHOCOLATE CHIP BROWNIES

A yummy recipe for your children to help you make for dessert or school lunches.

1/2 cup	soft butter or margarine	125 mL
1 cup	sugar	250 mL
2	eggs	2
1/2 teaspoon	vanilla	2 mL
1/2 cup	flour	125 mL
1 teaspoon	baking powder	5 mL
1/2 cup	cocoa	125 mL
1/3 cup	chocolate chips	75 mL
1/2 cup	chopped nuts (optional)	125 mL

1. Use a wooden spoon to combine butter and sugar. Stir until smooth. Add eggs and vanilla and mix well.

2. In a small bowl, combine flour, baking powder and cocoa. Stir this mixture into the egg mixture. Add chocolate chips and nuts and mix well.

3. Pour batter into a lightly greased 8-inch (20 cm) round or square microwave-safe baking dish and smooth the top. Microwave on Medium for 8 to 10 minutes, or until a toothpick inserted into the center of the brownies comes out clean. The top may still look soft. Let stand 5 minutes, then cool completely before cutting. Because of the chocolate chips in the batter, you don't need to put frosting on these brownies.

Makes 16 squares.

KIDS AND THE MICROWAVE

Δ Show them how all of the controls work.

Δ Stress that the microwave must never be operated empty.

Δ Show them which dishes can be used, and how to arrange the food on the dishes so that it cooks evenly.

Δ Instruct them to use oven mitts when removing cooked food from the microwave, as sometimes dishes become hot.

Δ Mention that food cooked in the microwave holds heat for a long time, so be careful to let it cool before eating.

Δ Cook with your child a few times until you are satisfied that he can cook safely by himself.

Regular Oven Method – CHOCOLATE- CHOCOLATE CHIP CUPCAKE CONES

Bake cones in a preheated 350° F (180° C) oven for 20 minutes, or until cones test done with a toothpick.

MICROWAVE HINT – CAKES

Let cake batter stand in the baking pan for 10 minutes before baking in the micro-wave. This allows the leavener to begin working.

CHOCOLATE-CHOCOLATE CHIP CUPCAKE CONES

When your child announces that she needs treats for the class party, make a batch of these cute cones. Top them with Microwave Fluffy Frosting (recipe on page 174) and they'll be a sure hit. If you're in a rush, use a cake mix instead of this batter.

3/4 cup	sugar	175 mL
1/4 cup	soft butter or margarine	50 mL
1	egg	1
2/3 cup	hot water	150 mL
1 cup	flour	250 mL
1/4 cup	cocoa	50 mL
3/4 teaspoon	baking soda	3 mL
1/2 teaspoon	salt	2 mL
1/2 teaspoon	vanilla	2 mL
1 cup	chocolate chips	250 mL
18 to 20	flat bottom ice cream cones	18 to 20
	Fluffy Frosting (recipe follows on page 172)	
	Chocolate chips or candy sprinkles to garnish	

1. Cream sugar and butter together with an electric mixer until light and fluffy. Beat in egg and hot water. Stir in flour, cocoa, baking soda and salt and blend until smooth. Stir in vanilla and chocolate chips.

2. Spoon 2 heaping tablespoons (25 mL) batter into each cone. Arrange 6 cones in a circle in the microwave. Microwave on High for 1 1/2 to 3 minutes, or until cake is firm to the touch. Cook remaining cones 6 at a time until all are cooked. Cool completely on a rack before frosting and decorating.

Variation: Spoon 2 tablespoons (25 mL) batter into muffin papers set in a microwave muffin pan. Microwave 6 cupcakes at a time on High for 2 to 3 minutes.

Makes 18 to 20 cone cupcakes.

MICROWAVE FLUFFY FROSTING

1 cup	sugar	250 mL
1/3 cup	water	75 mL
1/8 teaspoon	cream of tartar	0.5 mL
	Dash of salt	
2	egg whites	2
1/2 teaspoon	vanilla	2 mL

1. Combine sugar, water, cream of tartar and salt in an 8-cup (2 L) glass casserole or measure. Cover and microwave on High for 2 minutes. Stir, then microwave, uncovered, on High for 3 to 5 minutes, or until a soft ball forms when you drop a small amount of the mixture into cold water.

2. Beat egg whites until stiff. With mixer running, pour the hot sugar mixture into the egg whites in a slow, steady stream. Add vanilla after all syrup is added.

Makes enough frosting for 2 to 3 dozen cupcakes, or the top and sides of a layer cake.

Chocolate Pudding Cake

In response to a reader request, this is Margie Kreschollek's recipe for Chocolate Pudding Cake from *The Guaranteed Goof-Proof Microwave Cookbook*. It's yummy.

Cake:

2 tablespoons	butter	25 mL
1 cup	flour	250 mL
3/4 cup	sugar	175 mL
2 tablespoons	cocoa	25 mL
2 teaspoons	baking powder	10 mL
1/2 teaspoon	salt	2 mL
1/2 cup	milk	125 mL
1 teaspoon	vanilla	5 mL
1/2 cup	chopped nuts	125 mL

Pudding:

3/4 cup	brown sugar	175 mL
1/4 cup	cocoa	50 mL
1 1/4 cups	warm water	300 mL

1. Place butter in a small glass dish and microwave on High for 30 seconds or until melted.

2. Sift flour, sugar, cocoa, baking powder and salt into medium bowl. Stir in melted butter, milk, vanilla and nuts. Pour into a deep 9-inch (22 cm) round microwave-safe baking pan.

3. In a medium bowl, combine the pudding ingredients until well mixed. Pour over batter but do not stir.

4. Cover the pan loosely with waxed paper and microwave on High for 9 to 13 minutes. If your microwave doesn't have a turntable, rotate pan a half turn halfway through cooking if cake seems to be cooking unevenly.

5. Let stand, covered with waxed paper, for 10 minutes before serving. The pudding is thin at first, but thickens as the cake cools. Serve with sweetened whipped cream if desired.

Makes 6 servings.

Chocolate Hazelnut Mini Cheesecakes

Frangelico, the hazelnut liqueur used in this recipe, is available in 50 mL bottles, more than enough for this recipe.

Crust:

6 tablespoons	chocolate cookie crumbs	75 mL
2 tablespoons	melted butter	25 mL
3 tablespoons	ground hazelnuts	50 mL

Put muffin papers in the 6 holes of a microwave muffin pan, or into 6 custard cups. You will repeat this procedure, as the recipe makes at least 12 cheesecakes. Mix crust ingredients together and press about 2 teaspoons (10 mL) of the mixture into each paper. Set aside.

Filling:

4	1-ounce (28.5 g) squares semi-sweet chocolate	4
1	8-ounce (250 g) package cream cheese	1
1/3 cup	sugar	75 mL
1	egg	1
1/2 teaspoon	vanilla	2 mL
2 teaspoons	Frangelico hazelnut liqueur or other liqueur of your choice	10 mL
1/3 cup	sour cream	75 mL
	Dash of salt	

1. Melt chocolate in microwave on Medium-low for 3 to 5 minutes; stir twice.

2. Soften cream cheese in microwave on Low for 2 minutes.

3. Combine all filling ingredients until smooth, preferably with a food processor or electric mixer.

4. Pour filling over prepared crusts. Microwave 6 cheesecakes at a time on Medium for 4 minutes, or until set. Chill until firm.

Regular Oven Method – **Chocolate Hazelnut Cheesecakes**

Bake at 350° F (180° C) for 15 minutes, or until set.

GLAZE:

2	1-ounce (28.5 g) squares semi-sweet chocolate	2
2 tablespoons	whipping cream	25 mL
1 1/2 teaspoons	hazelnut or other liqueur	7 mL
12	whole hazelnuts to garnish	12

1. Melt chocolate in a small bowl on Medium-low for 3 to 4 minutes, stirring once. Add cream and liqueur and stir well.

2. Spread glaze on chilled cheesecakes (remove papers first if desired) and top each one with a whole hazelnut. Best made 1 to 3 days ahead. Can be frozen.

Makes about 12 servings.

CHOCOLATE PEANUT BUTTER ICE CREAM PIE

Chocolate and peanut butter make smooth partners in this ice cream pie. Use your microwave to melt the butter for the crust, soften the ice cream, melt honey crystals if necessary, for the filling, and to make the rich fudge-y sauce that you drizzle over each serving.

CRUST:

1/2 cup	melted butter or margarine	125 mL
2 cups	chocolate wafer crumbs	500 mL

FILLING:

6 cups	softened vanilla ice cream	1.5 L
1 cup	crunchy or smooth peanut butter	250 mL
1/2 cup	liquid honey	125 mL

SAUCE:

6	1-ounce (28.5 g) squares semi-sweet chocolate	6
3 tablespoons	whipping cream	50 mL
1 tablespoon	brandy (optional)	15 mL
1 tablespoon	hot coffee	15 mL
	Chopped salted peanuts to garnish	

1. To make crust: melt butter in a microwave-safe bowl in the microwave on High for 1 to 1 1/2 minutes, or until melted. Stir in crumbs. Press this mixture onto the bottom and halfway up the sides of a 9-inch (22 cm) springform pan. Refrigerate while you prepare the filling.

2. Soften ice cream in the microwave on Warm (your lowest setting) for 3 to 5 minutes, stirring occasionally. Combine ice cream with peanut butter and liquid honey using an electric mixer if possible. If honey has crystallized in the jar, microwave on High for 20 seconds at a time until no crystals remain. Time needed varies with quantity.

3. Spoon the ice cream mixture into the prepared crust and smooth the top. Cover tightly with plastic wrap and freeze until firm.

COOKING TIP – CHOCOLATE WAFER CRUST SUBSTITUTE:

Combine 1 1/2 cups (375 mL) graham wafer crumbs, 6 tablespoons (75 mL) cocoa and 6 tablespoons (75 mL) melted butter.

4. To make sauce: chop chocolate into small pieces and place in a large glass measuring cup. Microwave on Medium for 4 to 6 minutes, stirring each minute, until melted. Stir in cream, brandy and coffee. Cover and refrigerate.

5. Remove pie from freezer 1/2 hour before serving time and place it in the refrigerator. Reheat chocolate sauce on High for 1 to 2 minutes, or until heated through.

6. To serve: run a sharp knife around the sides of the pie, then remove the sides of the pan. Cut pie into serving pieces and drizzle warm chocolate sauce over each piece. Sprinkle the top of each piece with peanuts.

Makes 10 to 12 servings.

MICROWAVE HINT – MELTING CHOCOLATE

Chocolate can be melted in the microwave using High power. I prefer using Medium even though it takes a little longer. You are less likely to burn the chocolate using the lower power level. Stir chocolate often during melting so that you will know as soon as all pieces are melted; stopping the cooking at this point helps prevent scorching. You should never cover chocolate while melting it. Moisture which forms on the cover may drop into the chocolate, causing it to seize, or become dry and lumpy. It is almost impossible to save chocolate that has seized. A few drops of oil or shortening stirred quickly into the seized chocolate sometimes helps. Since water causes chocolate to seize, be sure that all utensils are perfectly dry.

CHOCOLATE PEANUT CLUSTERS

Make these with your children, then pack them into decorative jars or mugs for holiday giving.

1 3/4 cups	semi-sweet chocolate chips	425 mL
1 teaspoon	butter	5 mL
2 cups	salted Spanish peanuts	500 mL

1. Cover two baking sheets with waxed paper and set aside.

2. Place chocolate chips and butter in a large heatproof bowl. Microwave on Medium-low for 5 minutes, stirring every 2 minutes until melted. Add peanuts and stir well until nuts are well-coated with chocolate.

3. Drop chocolate mixture by teaspoonfuls (5 mL) onto the waxed paper-lined baking sheets. Refrigerate until chocolate is firm.

4. To store, place clusters between layers of waxed paper in a container with a tight fitting lid. Store in a cool place.

Makes 3 to 4 dozen clusters.

CHRISTMAS PUDDING

Christmas Pudding takes about 10 minutes to cook in the microwave, compared to 5 hours steaming on top of the stove. It benefits from a ripening period of several weeks to develop its rich flavour. If you make it early in the fall and refrigerate it, you can scratch it off the long list of things that have to be done closer to Christmas.

1 cup	muscat raisins	250 mL
1 cup	seedless raisins	250 mL
2 tablespoons	whiskey, brandy or fruit juice	25 mL
2 cups	finely chopped suet	500 mL
1 cup	dark brown sugar	250 mL
1 1/3 cups	fresh breadcrumbs	325 mL
1/3 cup	flour	75 mL
1/3 cup	mixed peel	75 mL
1 teaspoon	molasses	5 mL
1/2 teaspoon	salt	2 mL
1/2 teaspoon	cinnamon	2 mL
1/2 teaspoon	nutmeg	2 mL
1/4 teaspoon	cloves	1 mL
1/4 teaspoon	ginger	1 mL
1/2	orange, including both juice and grated rind	1/2
1/2	lemon, including both juice and grated rind	1/2
1/2	apple, peeled, seeded, finely chopped	1/2
3	eggs	3

1. Put muscats, raisins and whiskey in a small bowl. Mix well and let stand overnight.

2. The next morning, combine raisin mixture with all remaining ingredients except eggs. Stir in eggs one at a time, beating well after each addition.

3. Grease a 4-cup (1 L) pudding bowl. Fill it with the batter. Cover tightly with microwave-safe plastic wrap. Microwave on Medium for 10 to 12 minutes, or until toothpick inserted into center comes out clean. Uncover and cool pudding in the bowl.

4. Wrap cooled pudding well and store in a cool, dark place for several weeks to allow flavour to develop.

5. At serving time: Place pudding rounded side up on a microwave-safe serving plate and cover with plastic wrap or heatproof bowl. Microwave on Medium-high for 5 minutes, or until hot. Let stand, covered, for 3 minutes. Flame with warm brandy and serve with your favourite sauce.

Makes 1 large pudding, enough for 10 to 12 servings.

FOR INDIVIDUAL SERVING - SIZE CHRISTMAS PUDDINGS:

Spoon batter into buttered custard cups to 1/2-inch (1 cm) from the top edge. Arrange 6 cups in a circle in the microwave and microwave on High for 5 to 6 minutes, or until puddings test done with a wooden pick. Let stand 10 minutes before unmoulding.

MICROWAVE HINT – TESTING FOR DONENESS

To check if a dense food is warmed through to the center, insert a sharp knife into the food and hold it there for 10 seconds. If the blade is warm to the touch when you remove it, the food is warm also.

DATE SQUARES

An old-fashioned family favourite, updated for microwave cooking.

2 cups	chopped dates	500 mL
1/2 cup	corn syrup	125 mL
3/4 cup	water	175 mL
1/2 teaspoon	vanilla	2 mL
1 tablespoon	lemon juice	15 mL
1 1/3 cups	flour	325 mL
1 1/3 cups	lightly packed brown sugar	325 mL
1/2 teaspoon	baking soda	2 mL
1 1/3 cups	rolled oats	325 mL
2/3 cup	butter or margarine, melted	150 mL

1. For filling: Place dates, syrup, water, vanilla and lemon juice in an 8-cup (2 L) glass bowl or measuring cup.
Cover with plastic wrap and microwave on High for 6 to 7 minutes, or until dates are soft. Stir every two minutes. Let stand, covered, for 5 minutes, then uncover, stir, and cool for 15 minutes.

2. For top and bottom layers: Mix flour, brown sugar, soda and oats in a large bowl. Melt butter or margarine in a 2-cup (500 mL) glass measuring cup on High for about 1 minute, or until just melted. Stir in butter with a fork until mixture is crumbly.

3. Spoon half of the oat mixture into an 8-inch (20 cm) square microwave-safe pan and pat into a firm layer. Spread date filling over the oat layer, then top with remaining oat mixture. Pat topping down evenly.

4. Microwave on Medium-high for 10 minutes, or until filling bubbles.Let stand in baking dish until room temperature. Cut into squares and store in an airtight container.

Makes 25 squares.

MICROWAVE HINT

Remove lid from corn syrup, honey, or molasses bottle. Place glass bottle in microwave on High for 10 to 30 seconds (depending on quantity). The warm liquid will pour more quickly and easily. Honey which has crystallized can also be liquified in this manner.

Regular Oven Method – RHUBARB PIE

Bake at 450° F (230° C) for 15 minutes, then lower heat to 350° F (180° C) and bake for 40 to 45 minutes longer.

VARIATION

Substitute 1 cup (250 mL) fresh strawberries for 1 cup (250 mL) of the rhubarb for a deliciously sweet Strawberry Rhubarb Pie.

MICROWAVE HINT – PERFECTLY BAKED PIE IN 1/2 HOUR OR LESS

Prepare any 9-inch (22 cm) one or two-crust fruit or nut filing pie in a microwave-safe and heatproof pie plate. Make several slits in the top crust. Microwave on High for 8 to 10 minutes, or until the filling can be seen to bubble up through the slits in the crust. Transfer the partially baked pie to a preheated 425° F (220° C) oven and bake for 15 minutes, or until the crust is golden brown.

RHUBARB PIE

Toss a few strawberries into the rhubarb filling to make this springtime pie even rosier.

NO-FAIL PASTRY:

2/3 cup	lard	150 mL
1/3 cup	boiling water	75 mL
2 cups	cake and pastry flour	500 mL
3/4 teaspoon	salt	3 mL

1. Place lard in a large bowl and pour boiling water over. Stir vigorously with a fork or a whisk until lard melts and mixture is smooth.

2. Add flour and salt all at once and stir with a fork just until flour is mixed in. The dough will be very soft and sticky and must be refrigerated for at least 1/2 hour before rolling.

3. Roll half the dough into a circle large enough to line a 9-inch (22 cm) glass pie plate. Roll remaining dough to make the top crust when needed.

FILLING:

1/3 cup	all-purpose flour	75 mL
1 1/4 cup	sugar	300 mL
4 cups	rhubarb, cut into 1-inch (2 cm) pieces	1 L
	Granulated sugar (optional)	

1. Mix flour and sugar together, then combine with rhubarb in a large bowl. Spoon into prepared pastry-lined pan.

2. Roll remaining dough into a circle large enough to form the top crust for the pie. Place the pastry circle over the rhubarb, trim, seal and flute the edges. Cut several slits in the top crust and sprinkle lightly with granulated sugar if desired.

3. Preheat regular oven to 425° F (220° C)

4. First, microwave the pie on High for 8 to 10 minutes, or until filling begins to bubble up through the slits in the top crust.

5. Transfer pie to preheated oven and bake for 15 minutes, or until crust is golden.

6. Serve warm with sweetened whipped cream or vanilla ice cream.

Makes 1 pie, about 6 servings.

MY FAVOURITE APPLE PIE

I prefer to make this pie with Northern Spy or Granny Smith apples. They stay firm during baking and their flavour is delicious.

1 recipe	"No-Fail" Pastry (see Rhubarb Pie, page 181)	
1 tablespoon	flour	15 mL
1 cup	lightly packed brown sugar	250 mL
1/2 teaspoon	cinnamon	2 mL
	Dash of freshly grated nutmeg	
6 cups	sliced apples (about 7 large)	1.5 L

1. Line a 9-inch (22 cm) microwave-safe pie plate with pastry.

2. Stir flour, sugar and spices together, then toss well with apples.

3. Spoon apple mixture into the pastry-lined pan. Cover with top crust. Crimp and seal edges and cut several slits in the top crust to allow steam to escape. Sprinkle lightly with granulated sugar if desired.

4. Preheat regular oven to 425° F (220° C).

5. First microwave the pie on High for 8 to 10 minutes, or until filling begins to bubble. Transfer to preheated regular oven and bake for 15 minutes, or until the crust is golden.

6. Serve warm or at room temperature with vanilla ice cream or sharp cheddar cheese.

Makes 6 servings.

Regular Oven Method – MY FAVOURITE APPLE PIE

Bake at 450° F (230° C) for 15 minutes. Lower heat to 350° F (180° C) and bake for 45 minutes longer or until apples are tender.

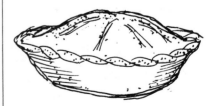

FLAMING MAPLE BANANAS

The maple syrup gives this tropical treat a truly Canadian twist.

1 tablespoon	butter	15 mL
3 tablespoons	maple syrup	50 mL
	Freshly grated nutmeg	
2	ripe bananas, peeled, cut in half	2
	lengthwise, then cut into chunks	
2 tablespoons	brandy	25 mL
	Vanilla ice cream	

1. Place butter, syrup and nutmeg in a microwave-safe pie plate. Microwave on High for 1 minute, or until butter melts. Stir to mix.

2. Arrange banana pieces on butter mixture, turning to coat with the mixture. Microwave on High for 1 to 1 1/2 minutes, or until bananas are heated through but still fairly firm.

3. Measure brandy into a 1-cup (250 mL) glass measure or small custard cup. Microwave on High for 10 seconds, or until just warm. If you overheat the brandy, you will burn off the alcohol and it will not ignite.

4. Pour warm brandy over bananas and ignite immediately. Spoon over ice cream.

Makes 2 servings.

MICROWAVE HINT – MAPLE SYRUP

Stir maple syrup into your microwave oatmeal for a yummy Canadian winter treat. Warm maple syrup in a microwave-safe jug before serving with pancakes, waffles or French toast. It will only take a few seconds on High to reach the desired temperature, so watch that it doesn't overheat.

FRUIT CRISP

Use one kind or a combination of several fruits, depending on what is in season or on hand in your refrigerator. Serve warm, plain, or topped with vanilla ice cream. This recipe is suitable for children to make with adult help.

4 cups	peeled chopped fruit (your choice of apples, pears, peaches, etc)	1 L
1/2 cup	flour	125 mL
1/4 cup	finely chopped nuts or sesame seeds (optional)	50 mL
1/2 cup	rolled oats	125 mL
	Dash cinnamon, ginger and nutmeg	
2/3 cup	brown sugar	150 mL
1/3 cup	soft butter or margarine	75 mL

l. Place fruit in a lightly buttered 8-inch (20 cm) round glass baking dish.

2. Mix remaining ingredients together in a small bowl using a fork. Sprinkle this mixture evenly over the fruit. Microwave on High for 6 minutes, or until fruit is tender. Let stand, uncovered, for 3 minutes before serving. If a crisp, brown top is desired, put the Fruit Crisp under the broiler for l minute, or until lightly browned. Watch carefully so that it doesn't burn.

Makes 4 servings.

GLAZED ALMONDS

A crunchy-sweet holiday gift idea. My mother makes these every Christmas.

1 tablespoon	butter	15 mL
1 tablespoon	corn syrup	15 mL
1/3 cup	sugar	75 mL
1 cup	whole blanched almonds	250 mL
	Salt	

1. Lightly butter a piece of foil and set aside.

2. Combine butter, corn syrup and sugar in a 4-cup (1 L) glass measure. Microwave on High for 1 to 2 minutes, or until sugar melts and mixture is smooth. Stir once during cooking.

3. Stir in almonds. Microwave on High for 3 to 4 minutes, or until almonds are a rich caramel colour. Stir once after 2 minutes.

4. Spread almond mixture in a single layer on lightly buttered foil and sprinkle lightly with salt. Cool and break into bitesize pieces.

5. Store at room temperature in an airtight container.

Makes about 2 cups (500 mL).

Vanilla Pudding

Use this pudding in desserts such as trifle, parfaits, or the Graham Squares dessert on page 187.

3 cups	milk	750 mL
6 tablespoons	cornstarch	75 mL
6 tablespoons	sugar	75 mL
	Dash of salt	
6 tablespoons	cold milk	75 mL
1 teaspoon	vanilla	5 mL

1. Place first amount of milk in a 4-cup (1 L) glass measure. Microwave on Medium for 7 to 9 minutes, or until scalded. If you wish to use a temperature probe to scald the milk, set the power level to Medium and the probe to 150° F (70° C).

2. Mix cornstarch, sugar and salt in a small bowl. Add the cold milk and stir to blend well.

3. Slowly stir the cornstarch mixture into the hot milk. Microwave on Medium for 3 to 4 minutes, or until pudding thickens. Stir twice during cooking.

4. Stir in vanilla. Chill before serving.

Makes 4 servings.

Chocolate Pudding

Use above recipe and stir 1/4 cup (50 mL) cocoa into cornstarch mixture. Increase sugar to 2/3 cup (150 mL). Keep all other ingredients and cooking steps the same as above.

Cooking Tip for Pudding

To prevent a skin from forming on the top of cooked pudding as it cools, press a piece of waxed paper or plastic wrap directly on the surface of the hot pudding. Chill. Remove paper just before serving.

GRAHAM SQUARES

Children love to help make this creamy dessert.

8 to 10	whole graham crackers	8 to 10
3 cups	milk	750 mL
6 tablespoons	cornstarch	75 mL
6 tablespoons	sugar	75 mL
	Dash of salt	
6 tablespoons	cold milk	75 mL
1 teaspoon	vanilla	5 mL
1 cup	whipping cream	250 mL
2 tablespoons	sugar	25 mL
	Few drops almond or vanilla extract	
1/2	of a 1-ounce (28.5 g) square semi-sweet chocolate	1/2

1. Place half of the graham crackers in a single layer to cover the bottom of an 8-inch (20 cm) square baking pan.

2. Place 3 cups (750 mL) milk in a 4-cup (1 L) glass measure. Microwave on Medium for 7 to 9 minutes, or until scalded. If you wish to use a temperature probe, set probe to 150° F (70° C) and use Medium power.

3. Mix cornstarch, sugar and salt in a small bowl. Add cold milk and stir to blend well.

4. Slowly stir cornstarch mixture into hot milk. Microwave on Medium for 3 to 4 minutes, or until pudding thickens. Stir twice during cooking. Stir in vanilla, then pour over crackers in baking pan. Refrigerate until cold.

5. Spread cold pudding evenly over crackers. Place another layer of crackers on top of pudding.

6. Whip cream, sugar and a few drops of almond or vanilla extract together. Spread whipped cream smoothly over crackers.

7. Grate chocolate over whipped cream. Cover tightly and refrigerate at least 4 hours or overnight before serving.

Makes 6 to 8 servings.

GRASSHOPPER PIE

In response to a reader request, Doris Grant, microwave cooking teacher with the Ottawa Board of Education, provided this recipe taken from one of her classes. She suggests varying the recipe by using 3 tablespoons (50 mL) Tia Maria in place of both liqueurs.

SHELL:

1 1/4 cups	fine chocolate wafer crumbs	300 mL
2 tablespoons	sugar (optional)	25 mL
1/4 cup	butter, melted	50 mL

FILLING:

24	large marshmallows	24
1/2 cup	milk	125 mL
1/4 cup	creme de menthe	50 mL
3 tablespoons	white creme de cacao	45 mL
1 1/2 cups	whipping cream, whipped	375 mL

1. Mix together the ingredients for the shell. Set aside 2 tablespoons (25 mL) of this crumb mixture to decorate the top of the pie. Press remaining mixture firmly and evenly into a 9-inch (22 cm) pie plate. Microwave on High for 2 to 2 1/2 minutes. Cool.

2. Place marshmallows and milk in a 3-quart (3 L) casserole. Microwave on High for 3 minutes, or until marshmallows can be blended with milk. Chill until cool and slightly thickened.

3. Stir liqueurs into marshmallow mixture, then fold in whipped cream.

4. Pour filling into crust and sprinkle with the reserved crumbs. Freeze or refrigerate until serving time.

Makes 1 pie.

LEMON CURD

Be sure to grate the rind from the lemon before cutting it in half to juice it. I learned the hard way how difficult it is to grate the rind of a squeezed lemon!

2	large eggs	2
1 cup	sugar	250 mL
1/2 cup	fresh lemon juice	125 mL
3 tablespoons	butter	50 mL
2 tablespoons	grated lemon rind	25 mL

1. Whisk eggs and sugar together until smooth. Whisk in lemon juice and stir in butter and grated rind. Microwave on High for 3 to 5 minutes, whisking every minute, until mixture boils and thickens.

2. Cool and store in the refrigerator.

3. To serve, spoon into baked tart shells and top with sweetened whipped cream.

Makes 1 1/2 cups (375 mL)

MICROWAVE HINT – GETTING MORE JUICE FROM CITRUS FRUIT

To get more juice from any citrus fruit, microwave on Medium for 1 minute before squeezing.

HAZELNUT FUDGE

The microwave simplifies an old-fashioned treat, still popular in the nineties.

4 cups	icing sugar	1 L
1/2 cup	unsweetened cocoa	125 mL
2 tablespoons	milk	25 mL
2 tablespoons	hazelnut liqueur(Frangelico)	25 mL
1/2 cup	butter	125 mL
3/4 cup	coarsely chopped hazelnuts	175 mL

1. Line an 8-inch (20 cm) square baking pan with waxed paper or plastic wrap.

2. Mix icing sugar and cocoa together in a large glass casserole. Add milk, liqueur and butter but do not stir. Microwave on High for 3 minutes.

3. Stir in hazelnuts. As soon as fudge begins to visibly thicken, quickly spread in prepared pan. Smooth the top. Chill until firm, then cut into small squares.

Makes 1 1/2 pounds (750 g) of fudge.

Microwave Hint for Cheesecake

If you wish to remove cheesecake from the baking dish before serving, line the dish with microwave-safe plastic wrap before filling and baking. Chill cheesecake thoroughly before attempting to remove from pan.

Microwave Baking Hint

Pies, cakes and cheesecakes will bake more evenly in the microwave if you elevate the baking dish 1 inch (2.5 cm). Use a heatproof plate or microwave rack to do this.

Lemon Cream Cheesecake

Make a day ahead to allow flavours time to blend, and serve with sliced fresh strawberries or a fresh berry sauce.

1/4 cup	butter or margarine, melted	50 mL
1 1/4 cups	graham cracker crumbs	300 mL
1/4 cup	sugar	50 mL
1	8-ounce (250 g) package cream cheese, softened	1
1/2 cup	sugar (second amount)	125 mL
1	egg	1
1/4 teaspoon	vanilla	1 mL
1 teaspoon	lemon zest	5 mL
2 tablespoons	lemon juice	25 mL
3/4 cup	sour cream	175 mL
	Sliced fresh strawberries to garnish	
	Mint leaves to garnish	
	Lemon Zest to garnish	

1. Mix melted butter, crumbs and 1/4 cup (50 mL) sugar together and press onto the bottom and sides of a 9-inch (22 cm) glass pie plate. Microwave on High for 1 1/2 minutes. Set aside.

2. Combine cream cheese, 1/2 cup (125 mL) sugar, egg, vanilla, zest and lemon juice, and stir until smooth.

3. Stir in sour cream. Pour into prepared shell and smooth the top. Microwave on Medium for 8 to 10 minutes, or until the center is just set. Cool slightly, then cover and refrigerate until cold. Prepare to this point a day ahead, if possible.

4. To serve, decorate cheesecake with fresh sliced strawberries, or other fruit, mint leaves and lemon zest. Drizzle each serving with Raspberry Coulis (see Charlotte Russe, page 166-67) if desired.

Makes 8 servings.

LUSCIOUS LEMON CREAM PIE

Montreal food writer Norene Gilletz suggested that I share this delicious recipe with my readers. It is from *The Microwave Bible*, formerly called *MicroWays*, a very comprehensive and practical microwave cookbook.

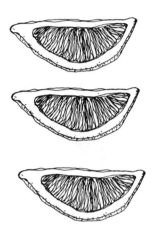

1	9-inch (22 cm) graham wafer crust	1
3/4 cup	sugar	175 mL
1/4 cup	cornstarch	50 mL
1 cup	water	250 mL
1 teaspoon	grated lemon rind	5 mL
1/3 cup	lemon juice	75 mL
2	egg yolks	2
1/4 pound	cream cheese or pot cheese (dry cottage cheese)	125 g
2	egg whites	2
2 tablespoons	sugar (2nd amount)	25 mL
1 cup	whipping cream plus 2 tablespoons (25 mL) icing sugar (optional) Grated lemon rind	250 mL

1. Combine 3/4 cup (175 mL) sugar with cornstarch, water, lemon rind and lemon juice. Whisk to blend. Add yolks and mix well. Microwave, uncovered, on High for 4 to 5 minutes, until thick and bubbling.

2. Cut cream cheese into chunks and add to lemon mixture. Mix until cheese is melted and mixture is well blended. Place a piece of waxed paper directly onto the surface of the mixture to prevent a skin from forming. Chill until cold.

3. Beat egg whites to soft peaks. Gradually add 2 tablespoons (25 mL) sugar. Beat until stiff. Fold into chilled lemon mixture. Pour into crust. Refrigerate 2 to 3 hours, until set.

4. Whip cream and icing sugar together until stiff. Pipe through a pastry bag onto pie. Sprinkle with grated lemon rind. Pie can be made up to 2 days ahead, but garnish the day you are serving it. Do not freeze.

Makes 6 servings.

MICROWAVE HINT FROM NORENE GILLETZ

When making soups, sauces and beverages, place a microwave-safe pie plate under the cooking container to catch boil-overs and eliminate messy clean-ups.

Nanaimo Bars

When I was little, my Aunt Mina made these and called them "Chunkies," because that's what you'd become if you ate too many! They're still a family favourite at holiday time.

Base:

1/2 cup	butter	125 mL
1/4 cup	sugar	50 mL
5 tablespoons	cocoa	75 mL
1	egg	1
1 teaspoon	vanilla	5 mL
1 2/3 cups	graham wafer crumbs	400 mL
1 cup	coconut	250 mL
1/2 cup	chopped walnuts	125 mL

1. Place butter in a large glass measure and microwave on High for 1 minute, or until melted. Stir in sugar, cocoa, egg and vanilla. Microwave on Medium for 1 minute, or until slightly thickened. Stir once during cooking.

2. Stir in crumbs, coconut and walnuts. Press firmly into a lightly buttered 9-inch (22 cm) square pan. Chill until filling is ready.

Filling:

1/4 cup	butter, softened	50 mL
2 cups	icing sugar	500 mL
1	egg*	1

1. Cream butter until smooth. Gradually stir in icing sugar, then stir in egg. Spread over base and chill for 30 minutes.

Topping:

4	1-ounce (28.5 g) squares semi-sweet chocolate	4
1 tablespoon	butter	15 mL

1. Place chocolate and butter in a 1-cup (250 mL) glass measure. Microwave on Medium for 2 1/2 to 3 minutes, or until melted. Stir once during melting.

2. Spread topping on chilled filling layer. Chill well. When chocolate is set, cut into small squares. Wrap and store in the refrigerator.

Makes 25 small squares.

Substitution:

* Substitute milk or cream for egg if desired. Add just enough to make mixture smooth and easy to spread over crust.

Nutty Caramel Corn

A buttery treat for anyone on your gift list. Choose optional ingredients according to the age and tastes of the recipients. If children are making the Caramel Corn, they will need adult help, as the syrup is hot.

l cup	sugar	250 mL
1/2 cup	corn syrup	125 mL
1/3 cup	butter	75 mL
10 cups	popped corn	2.5 L

Choose l cup (250 mL) of 2 or 3 of the following:

Δ toasted blanched almonds   Δ pecan halves
Δ cashew pieces   Δ chopped dried apricots
Δ small gumdrops   Δ mini marshmallows
Δ chopped jujubes   Δ candied cherry halves
Δ small jelly beans

l. Grease a jelly roll pan and set aside.

2. Combine sugar, corn syrup, and butter in a 4-cup (l L) glass measure. Microwave on High for l 1/2 minutes, or until butter melts. Stir, then microwave on High for l 1/2 to 2 minutes more, or until slightly thickened. Stir each minute.

3. Mix popcorn and optional ingredients of your choice in a large bowl. Pour in the butter mixture and stir to mix well. Spread this mixture on the prepared baking sheet, and sprinkle lightly with salt if desired.

4. Cool then store in a sealed plastic bag, jar or tin.

Makes 12 cups (3 L).

Microwave Hint

When you are boiling food in a bowl or casserole in the microwave, always use oven mitts to lift it out. The heat from the cooking food transfers to the container to make it hot.

Regular Oven Method – OATMEAL LEMON SQUARES

Bake base in a preheated 350° F (180° C) oven for 10 minutes. Combine all regular oven filling ingredients except icing sugar and whisk until smooth.

Pour over baked base and bake at 350° F (180° C) for 15 to 20 minutes, or until golden brown on top. Cool, then cut into squares and sprinkle with icing sugar.

OATMEAL LEMON SQUARES

This is a good recipe for your child to make for dessert.

BASE:

1/2 cup	flour	125 mL
1/2 cup	brown sugar	125 mL
2/3 cup	rolled oats	150 mL
1/3 cup	butter, melted	75 mL

FILLING FOR MICROWAVE VERSION:

	Grated rind & juice of 1 lemon	
2	eggs	2
2/3 cup	sugar	150 mL
2 teaspoons	cornstarch	10 mL
1/2 teaspoon	baking powder	2 mL
	Icing sugar (optional)	

FILLING FOR REGULAR OVEN VERSION:

2 tablespoons	flour	25 mL
3	medium eggs	3
1 cup	sugar	250 mL
1/2 teaspoon	baking powder	2 mL
	Juice and grated rind of 1 large lemon	
	Icing sugar	

1. To make base: Combine flour, sugar, oats and butter in a small bowl. Stir in melted butter. Press this mixture to form a firm layer in a buttered 8-inch (20 cm) square or round baking pan. Microwave on High for 1 minute.

2. For microwave filling: Combine all microwave filling ingredients except icing sugar in a medium bowl and beat with a whisk or spoon until smooth. Pour over base and microwave on High for 4 to 6 minutes, or until filling is set in the center. Cover with waxed paper and cool completely before cutting into squares. Sprinkle with icing sugar.

Makes 6 to 8 servings.

ORANGE CHEESECAKE FOR TWO

Making this very small cheesecake will help you to resist the temptation of finishing a larger one!

3 tablespoons	graham wafer crumbs	50 mL
1 tablespoon	sugar	15 mL
1 tablespoon	butter, melted	15 mL
1	small package (125 g) cream cheese, softened	1
1 tablespoon	sugar (second amount)	15 mL
	Grated zest of 1 orange	
2 teaspoons	orange liqueur or juice	10 mL
1	egg	1
2 tablespoons	light sour cream	25 mL
2 teaspoons	orange marmalade	10 mL
	Orange slices or other fresh fruit to garnish	

1. Combine graham wafer crumbs, 1 tablespoon (15 mL) sugar and butter in a small bowl. Press onto the bottom of a microwave-safe 4 1/2-inch (11 cm) tart or quiche dish, 3 muffin cups, or 3 custard cups. Microwave on High for 1 minute.

2. Combine cream cheese, 1 tablespoon (15 mL) sugar, orange zest and liqueur or juice, and egg. Pour over baked shells. Microwave on Medium for 2 to 3 minutes, or until filling is set.

3. Combine sour cream and marmalade and spread on top of baked cheesecakes. Microwave on High for 1 minute. Cool cheesecakes on counter to room temperature, then cover and refrigerate until cold. At serving time, garnish with fresh fruit, if desired.

Makes 2 to 3 servings.

MICROWAVE HINT FOR SINGLES

If you have a favourite casserole that you seldom make because it's too large, why not freeze individual servings in yogurt or margarine containers? Transfer to a microwave-safe container before defrosting and reheating in the microwave. Treat yourself well – you're worth it!

Regular Oven Method – PUMPKIN CHEESECAKE

Bake at 300° F (150° C) for 45 minutes to 1 hour or until almost set. Spread sour cream mixture on cake and bake for 5 minutes more.

RECIPE FOR PUMPKIN PIE SPICE

Stir together 2 teaspoons (10 mL) cinnamon, 1 teaspoon (5 mL) nutmeg, 1 teaspoon (5 mL) ground ginger and 1/2 teaspoon (2 mL) ground cloves. Store extra in a sealed jar.

PUMPKIN CHEESECAKE

A delicious finale for the Halloween pumpkin. Freeze extra cooked pumpkin purée for another cheesecake.

1 cup	graham cracker crumbs	250 mL
1/4 cup	finely chopped pecans	50 mL
2 tablespoons	sugar	25 mL
	Dash of pumpkin pie spice [recipe below]	
1/4 cup	butter, melted	50 mL
2/3 cup	cottage cheese	150 mL
1	large egg	1
1	8-ounce (250 g) package cream cheese, softened	1
1/3 cup	sugar	75 mL
1 tablespoon	flour	15 mL
1/2 teaspoon	orange zest	2 mL
1 teaspoon	pumpkin pie spice [recipe below]	5 mL
	Dash salt	
3/4 cup	cooked puréed pumpkin	175 mL
1/3 cup	sour cream	75 mL
2 teaspoons	orange marmalade	10 mL
	Thinly sliced orange to garnish	

1. In a small bowl combine crumbs, pecans, sugar and a dash of pumpkin pie spice. Add butter and mix well. Press onto bottom and sides of a buttered 9-inch (22 cm) microwave-safe pie plate or quiche dish. Set aside.

2. Purée cottage cheese and egg in food processor or blender. Add cream cheese, sugar, flour, zest, pumpkin pie spice and salt and purée until smooth.

3. Stir pumpkin into cheese mixture. Pour into shell and smooth top. Microwave on Medium for 10 to 12 minutes or until almost set.

4. Combine sour cream and marmalade. Spread on baked cheesecake. Microwave on Medium for 1 1/2 minutes more. Cool to room temperature then cover and refrigerate overnight.

5. Serve garnished with orange slices. Can refrigerate up to 1 week.

Makes 6 to 8 servings.

PUMPKIN PIE

In her book, *Master Your Microwave*, Glenda James provides this tasty version of a Thanksgiving favourite. I have changed the spice amounts slightly to satisfy the pumpkin pie fanatics in my family.

1 1/2 cups	cooked, pureed pumpkin	375 mL
1 teaspoon	flour	5 mL
1 teaspoon	cornstarch	5 mL
1/3 cup	brown sugar	75 mL
1/2 teaspoon	cinnamon	2 mL
1/4 teaspoon	nutmeg	1 mL
	Dash of ground cloves and salt	
1	egg	1
2/3 cup	milk	150 mL
1	9-inch (22 cm) pastry shell, baked in a glass pie plate	1

1. Mix all filling ingredients in a medium bowl with a whisk or electric mixer. Pour into prepared shell. Microwave on Medium for14 to 16 minutes, or until set.

2. Chill before serving, and serve with sweetened whipped cream.

Makes 6 servings.

MICROWAVE HINT – COOKING PUMPKIN

To cook fresh pumpkin in the microwave, cut the pumpkin in half, scoop the seeds out and place cut side down on a microwave plate. If pumpkin is small enough to fit in the microwave whole, cut several slits in it with a sharp knife before cooking to allow steam to escape. Microwave on High for 6 to 7 minutes per pound, or until soft. Remove skin (and seeds if whole) and purée pulp until smooth.

RICE PUDDING

When you cook rice in milk in the microwave, it usually boils over during cooking. To avoid this messy problem, it is easier to cook the rice first, then combine it with a rich egg custard, also made in the microwave. The pudding below, made in this manner, is creamy, rich and delicious.

1/2 cup	raisins	125 mL
	Boiling water	
3 tablespoons	cornstarch	50 mL
1/3 to 1/2 cup	sugar	75 to 125 mL
2 cups	milk	500 mL
	Dash of salt	
2	egg yolks	2
1 teaspoon	vanilla	5 mL
2 cups	cooked long grain rice	500 mL

1. Place raisins in a small bowl and add enough boiling water to cover. Let stand for 30 minutes, then drain well. Set aside.

2. Stir cornstarch and sugar together in a 4-cup (1 L) glass bowl or measure. Gradually stir in milk and salt. Microwave on Medium for 9 to 10 minutes, or until thickened. Whisk or stir every 3 minutes.

3. Beat yolks in a small bowl. Whisk in a small amount of the hot mixture, then whisk the warmed yolks back into the milk mixture. Microwave on Medium for 1 minute.

4. Stir in vanilla, cooked rice and raisins. Serve warm or chilled.

Makes 6 servings.

TARTE TATIN

The apple filling for this upside-down French tarte is cooked in the microwave. After the crust is set in place on the apples, it is placed in a hot oven to brown and crisp the crust. Use Granny Smiths, Northern Spies, or other firm cooking apple for best results.

| 1 | recipe sweet butter pastry for a 1-crust pie, chilled | 1 |

FILLING:

5 cups	peeled, thinly sliced apples	1.25 L
1 tablespoon	lemon juice	15 mL
1/2 to 2/3 cups	brown sugar	125 to 150 mL
2 tablespoons	butter	25 mL
1 tablespoon	water	15 mL
2 teaspoons	lemon juice	10 mL
1/4 teaspoon	freshly grated nutmeg	1 mL
1/2 teaspoon	cinnamon	2 mL
1 teaspoon	lemon zest	5 mL

GLAZE:

3 tablespoons	apricot preserves	50 mL
2 teaspoons	brandy	10 mL
1 1/2 teaspoons	water	7 mL

SAUCE:

1/2 cup	dairy sour cream	125 mL
4 teaspoons	icing sugar	20 mL
1/4 teaspoon	vanilla	1 mL

1. Roll pastry into a circle slightly larger than the diameter of the microwave-safe pie plate you will use. Set aside.

2. Place apple slices in a large bowl of cold water with 1 tablespoon (15 mL) lemon juice to keep them from browning. Drain and pat dry before using.

3. Butter a 9-inch (22 cm) microwave-safe, ovenproof pie plate. Place brown sugar, butter and water in it. Microwave on High for 30 seconds to melt butter. Stir to mix well, then microwave on High for 1 to 2 minutes more, or until mixture boils and smells like caramel.

4. Arrange drained apple slices in a decorative pattern on sugar mixture. (Remember that the pie will be inverted for serving, and the bottom will become the top.) Sprinkle apples with 2 teaspoons (10 mL) lemon juice, nutmeg, cinnamon, and lemon zest. Cover with microwave-safe plastic wrap and microwave on High for 4 to 6 minutes, or until apples are tender.

5. Place pastry over apples and trim to fit pan. Cut a steam vent in pastry, then bake in a preheated 425° F (220° C) oven for 15 to 20 minutes, or until crust is brown.

6. Cool in the pan for 10 minutes, then invert onto a serving plate. If any apple slices stick to the pan, lift them off and set them in place on the tarte.

7. Place glaze ingredients in a 1-cup glass measure and microwave on High for 1 minute, or until melted and hot. Press through a sieve, then brush smooth glaze over the hot, inverted tarte.

8. Mix sauce ingredients together and spoon over individual servings of warm tarte. If desired, pass sweetened whipped cream instead of the sauce.

Makes 6 servings.

Sour Cream Peach Pie

Make your favourite peach pie in a glass pie plate and cut the cooking time in half with microwave help. This Sour Cream Peach Pie is a favourite of mine.

	Pastry for a single crust 9-inch(22cm) pie	
5 cups	peeled, sliced peaches	1.25 L
1/3 cup	flour	75 mL
2/3 cup	brown sugar	150 mL
1 cup	dairy sour cream	250 mL
1 tablespoon	brown sugar to garnish	15 mL

1. Line a 9-inch (22 cm) glass pie plate with pastry. Arrange peach slices in shell in an attractive pattern.

2. Beat together flour, 2/3 cup (150 mL) brown sugar and sour cream until smooth. Pour over peaches.

3. Preheat regular oven to 425° F (220° C).

4. Microwave the pie on High for 8 minutes, or until filling is hot and bubbly in a 2-inch (5 cm) border. Sprinkle brown sugar garnish over pie, then transfer to preheated oven. Bake for 10 to 15 minutes, or until pastry and filling are golden brown. Serve warm or at room temperature.

Makes 6 to 8 servings.

Microwave Hint – Peeling Peaches

Place 4 cups (1 L) hot water in a large glass bowl. Microwave on High for 8 minutes, or until water boils. Place 3 ripe peaches in water and let stand for 2 minutes. Remove fruit and cool in cold water. The skin will slip off easily. Repeat the procedure until all fruit is peeled.

CHOCOLATE COVERED BANANAS

Several summers ago, while on holidays, I enjoyed a chocolate-covered banana for the first time. I have since made these delectable treats at home and recommend that you try them too.

2	large bananas	2
1 1/2 ounces	semi-sweet or milk chocolate	45 g

TOPPINGS:
crushed chocolate covered English
toffee, chopped nuts, or coconut.

1. Melt chocolate in a microwave-safe bowl on Medium for 1 minute. Stir to check, as chocolate retains its solid shape even when melted.

2. Cut banana in half and stick popsicle sticks into the cut ends. Coat the entire banana with melted chocolate, then sprinkle crushed candy, chopped nuts or coconut all over the chocolate before it hardens.

3. Place bananas on waxed paper on a plate in the freezer. Once they are frozen, wrap and store in the freezer, or, if you're like me, eat them right away!

Makes 2 servings.

MICROWAVE HINT FOR EASIER CLEAN-UP

If toffee left in a glass measuring cup or bowl is difficult to remove, fill cup with hot water and microwave on High to boiling. The toffee will melt and the container will be easy to wash.

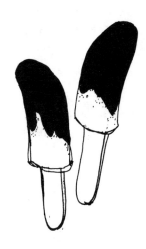

TRIPLE FRUIT PIE

When I tasted this prize-winning pie during the *Ottawa Citizen* Recipe Contest judging, I could hardly wait to try it again. In fact, I decided not to wait until berry season, but used frozen berries (defrosted in the microwave) and fresh peaches, and adapted the recipe so that the pie is baked in half the time using both microwave and regular ovens.

| 1 | 9-inch (22 cm) pie shell, in a deep, microwave-safe, ovenproof pie plate | 1 |

FILLING:

3 cups	blueberries	750 mL
3 cups	peeled, sliced peaches	750 mL
1 1/2 cups	raspberries	375 mL
3/4 cup	sugar	175 mL
1/2 teaspoon	cinnamon	2 mL
1/4 teaspoon	nutmeg	1 mL
2 tablespoons	cornstarch	25 mL

TOPPING:

1/2 cup	butter, softened	125 mL
1 cup	flour	250 mL
1 cup	brown sugar	250 mL

1. To partially bake pie shell in the microwave: Place a piece of waxed paper in pie shell and fill shell with pie weights, dried beans or uncooked rice. Place in freezer for 10 minutes, then microwave on High for 3 minutes. Remove weights and paper from shell.

2. If frozen fruit is used, defrost in the microwave in a colander set over a bowl so that the juice will drain off. Combine drained or fresh fruits together, then spoon into partially baked pie shell.

3. Mix together sugar, cinnamon, nutmeg and cornstarch and sprinkle evenly over fruit.

4. Blend topping ingredients until crumbly and sprinkle over fruit. Set pie plate on a microwave-safe, ovenproof tray in the microwave (this pie tends to bubble over) and microwave on High for 8 to 10 minutes, or until bubbly. Transfer pie and tray to preheated 425° F (220° C) oven and bake for 10 to 12 minutes, or until crust and topping are golden brown.

Makes 6 to 8 servings.

The Best of NEW WAVE COOKING INDEX

* indicates recipes which include regular oven method

INDEX OF HELPFUL HINTS AND HOW–TO'S

INDEX OF FAST AND EASY RECIPES FOR YOUNG, INEXPERIENCED AND OCCASIONAL COOKS

* indicates recipes which include regular oven method

Published by
Creative Bound Inc.
P.O. Box 424, Carp, Ontario
Canada K0A 1L0

ISBN 0-921165-20-X
Printed and bound in Canada
© 1992 Pam Collacott

Book Design: Wendelina O'Keefe
Cover Photo: Photograhic Illustrations, Ottawa, Ontario

Canadian Cataloguing in Publication Data

Collacott, Pam, 1947 –
    The best of new wave cooking

Includes index.
ISBN 0-921165-20-X

    1. Microwave cookery.   I. Title

TX832.C64 1992   641.5'882   C92-090253-7

Cover foods, clockwise from top:
Pasta with Sausage & Pepper Sauce; Date Squares; Nanaimao Bars; Chocolate Butter Crunch; Caramel Flans; Beef Stew with Herb Dumplings

The Best of NEW WAVE COOKING

• PAM COLLACOTT •